BEHIND THE MAS

BEHIND THE MASK
TYSON FURY

MY AUTOBIOGRAPHY

CENTURY

1 3 5 7 9 10 8 6 4 2

Century
20 Vauxhall Bridge Road
London SW1V 2SA

Century is part of the Penguin Random House group of companies
whose addresses can be found at global.penguinrandomhouse.com.

Copyright © Tyson Fury 2019

Tyson Fury has asserted his right under the Copyright, Designs and
Patents Act, 1988, to be identified as the author of this work.

First published by Century in 2019

www.penguin.co.uk

A CIP catalogue record for this book is available from the British Library.

Hardback ISBN 9781529124866

Trade Paperback ISBN 9781529124873

Typeset in 15/19.25pt Perpetua by Jouve (UK), Milton Keynes
Printed and bound in Great Britain by Clays Ltd, Elcograf S.p.A.

Penguin Random House is committed to a sustainable future for our
business, our readers and our planet. This book is made from
Forest Stewardship Council® certified paper.

This book is dedicated to the cause of mental health awareness. I would plead with anyone reading my story who feels they are experiencing similar issues to seek out professional help immediately. There is hope.

ACKNOWLEDGEMENTS

I want to thank my wife Paris for putting up with all of the rubbish that I've made her deal with, and to thank her for all of her goodness and kindness.

CONTENTS

PROLOGUE

June 2016, Manchester

The speedometer hit 160mph. This was it – the end was coming, the pain would be over.

The sun was shining on a perfect summer's day. I had just picked up a brand-new red convertible Ferrari; I was the heavyweight champion of the world; I had a beautiful wife and family. My life should have been as good as it gets, but my soul was as black as my boots.

Just a few months previously I was standing in the ring with the world acclaiming me as the best heavyweight on earth. I was the man who had followed in the footsteps of such legends as Jack Dempsey, Muhammad Ali, Mike Tyson and Lennox Lewis. Yet now, as I drove along the motorway in this new dream car, I was caught in the nightmare of clinical depression. I had it all but I felt I had nothing to live for. There was no point to my existence.

As I came off the motorway and slowed down I just knew it was time to leave all this torture behind. Right, come on, Tyson, just get this over with. My mind was made up, it was in a place of meaninglessness. Nothing mattered; I didn't matter. I looked at the upcoming bridge. That was the target; that was the end point. The Ferrari's engine roared back into life. It would be the last sound I would hear. In a couple of seconds my mind would be clear, devoid of all the voices that were boiling in my head. I put my foot to the floor. The end was in view.

Then, in the moment before I was set to crash, a voice shot into my head: 'No! Stop! Think about your kids!' And I blasted past the bridge before hammering on the brakes.

· · ·

That's as close as I have come to ending it all. I look back with relief and bewilderment at just how a person can enter such a state, suffocated by depression like I was, and I give thanks to God. Without my faith I would have committed suicide that day. My children would not have a father to guide them and my amazing wife Paris would have been robbed of a husband who, for all my faults, loves her with all his heart.

Unless you have experienced it, you really don't know what depression is like. At that moment, and in other moments like it, I have just felt like nothing on earth matters; absolutely nothing. So what is the point of living? Immediately after I got out of the car I was thinking about what the consequences could have been, and I don't want to go anywhere near that point again in my life. But then it is very easy to slowly slip back into that way of thinking. I'm sure some who are reading this may have experienced what I'm describing. I want to assure everyone that there is a way out, there is a pathway to receiving help. If that wasn't the case I wouldn't have made my comeback, I wouldn't be fighting again in the hardest sport in the world. I could easily have ended up in a padded cell because of some of the things I have done, but I'm fighting back.

1 December 2018, the Staples Center, Los Angeles

'You're beat, you're beat. I'm going to take you to school, you big dosser.' As we were brought together before the first bell, and throughout the first round, I was taunting the WBC heavyweight champion Deontay Wilder. But in the opening moments of the fight I did find out why Wilder calls himself 'Bomb Squad'. He landed a jab and I thought, 'Woah.' I could feel the knuckle right through my hand as I blocked it.

Before the fight my trainer Ben Davison had been concerned about the way in which Wilder often hits guys with punches behind the head, which can have a devastating effect on the brain. Ben had actually flagged it up to referee Jack Reiss and as the fight wore on, he was wary of how Wilder was trying to catch me. In the ninth round Ben's fear became a reality. Wilder tagged me behind the ear and down I went. Maybe I got a little too comfortable and the effects of losing so much weight before the fight had taken a little spring out of my step. But it's also the kind of shot that short-circuits the brain. There's nothing you can do when you get hit behind the ear or on the temple: your body loses control and you hit the deck. Still, whatever, I was down, and with two minutes left in the round Wilder believed he had enough time to finish me off.

Wrong! I wasn't hurt and I got to my feet and got back to what I had been doing – and that was boxing the head off Wilder. As he came at me, winging right hands, I clamped him to my body, allowed my head to clear and then I fired back. Soon I was snapping his head back with my jab, a shot I had honed as a weapon back in my earliest days as an amateur. Wilder didn't know what to do with me. He's the WBC champion, with scary power in his fists, but he can't land his punches. He can't get control of me the way he did with the rest of his thirty-nine opponents, all dispatched by knockout. I finished the round strongly, slam bam in his face with solid shots. How frustrating must that have been for him? He was used to having opponents on the hook and then taking them out.

While I was showing a surprised Wilder that I was going nowhere, little did I know that Ben was having a furious row with the local officials who were trying to keep him from getting to his feet to see if I was all right. The rule in LA is that the corner must remain seated, but when the heavyweight championship of the world is on the line that's easier said than done. Ben desperately wanted to know what kind of shape I was in. But with under a minute to go I was in my groove, firing home my jab, and Wilder was now the one looking tired, unable to sustain any attacks as I taunted him by putting my hands behind my back and sticking my tongue out at him.

At the start of the tenth round I was on my toes and rapped Wilder's chin with a quick one-two. He had put so much into trying to stop me in the ninth he was tiring, and I was taking the fight to him. He was now content to sit back and try to land one big final right hand. That allowed me to easily outwork him. There was no way I was going to fall into that trap. With just under a minute to go I sent a right hand of my own thudding into his face and I smartly moved out of range. That drew a big 'ooh' from the crowd, and then I showed my defensive skills as I slipped about five blows just before the sound of the bell. He hadn't landed a decent punch the whole three minutes, and as the bell sounded we were in a clinch. I gave him a few more verbals and stuck my tongue out at him again.

5

He trudged back to his corner and I went back to mine with a new spring in my step and screamed at the crowd, 'Come on!' Then I shouted at Ben, 'I'm the Gypsy King, I will be victorious.' I was reaffirming my confidence and belief that I was in the middle of making history, writing a script that few thought was possible. At ringside the BT Sport commentator John Rawling was saying it was 'a performance to make the hairs on the back of your neck stand up'. Ben told me that I had to give more than I had ever given in my life, that I had to keep my composure and go out and steal the last two rounds. 'Don't take any silly chances.' But I had to do enough to take my chances when they came. I did exactly that – and a bit more – in the eleventh round, at the end of which I pumped out my fist to the fans and the world to proclaim that I was on the cusp of the greatest comeback in boxing history.

Just ninety-six seconds later the dream died. I was gone. Wilder detonated a right hand and then landed a free left hook as I was going down. I hit the canvas with an almighty crash. This had to be the end, thought Wilder and everybody else in the arena, and the millions watching around the world on TV . . .

INTRODUCTION

Forgive me, Father, for I have sinned.

My name is Tyson Luke Fury and, like everyone else in this world, I'm a flawed character. I suffer from mental health issues, I have obsessive compulsive disorder. I also happen to be the number one heavyweight boxer in the world.

My journey so far in this life has never been dull. From the moment I was born three months prematurely, I found myself in a fight for survival. And for as long as I can remember I have always felt that I have a natural ability for sport and particularly boxing, which started off in the kitchen with my brother Shane, when we would wrap towels across our fists and punch each other until we were exhausted. My achievements in the ring have been there for all to see, but as a teenager I used to play golf a lot, right up until I was about twenty-one and had an eight handicap. I'll still go out from time to time and just for fun at the range I'll hit a golf ball 250 yards with one hand. I've always found that with every sport I can handle myself, whether it is clay pigeon shooting, basketball, rowing or anything. But my life was always going to be absorbed by boxing. This was my gift; this was the path that had been given to me. It feels like it has been my birthright to be an elite fighting man. It's part of my DNA. In previous generations, there were members of the Fury family who had been successful bare-knuckle fighters. Now we're professional boxers, like my father John, who boxed as well as having some bare-knuckle fights, and my half-brother Tommy, who's looking to be a hit in the ring after his time on *Love Island*.

The ring would be the arena in which I would show my sporting greatness and honour the family name. But the boxing business would also help bring my downfall – and then open the path again to my rise from the depths of despair.

· · ·

When I first started writing this book I weighed 28 stone, was drinking heavily, hated boxing and was battling a deep depression. I had no interest in returning to boxing. At that point, all I could see and feel in my life was pain. The belts, the acclaim of becoming the heavyweight champion of the world – the fulfilment of a life-long dream in 2015 – had only left a cold, hollow feeling inside that wouldn't leave me. It had meant absolutely nothing.

Two years later, I have been recognised by the prestigious American boxing magazine *The Ring* as the top man in the heavyweight division. I'm fitter than I have ever been and happier than ever before, with a real purpose to living, even though I am constantly reminded that my underlying issues with mental health will never go away.

Throughout my life I have battled anxiety, and between November 2015 and October 2017 I descended into a vile pit of despair but found a way back to having a life again. After only two comeback fights in 2018 I went on to face WBC heavyweight champion Deontay Wilder. I shocked the world with how I performed, winning in the eyes of everyone except two of the judges at ringside, with one scoring it a draw and the other giving it to Wilder.

Some will think they know me from some of my past comments on social media, others will simply focus on my boxing career, but I hope this book will reveal to everyone who I am, my true personality, what I have gone through in my life, and my ongoing struggles.

In the Bible there is a character called Job, who was one of the wealthiest men in the world and then he lost it all, everything he had. He was tormented and even his closest friends turned against him and pressurised him to deny God. But he stood firm and God eventually blessed him with more than he had ever had – and that in many ways is my story. At twenty-seven years of age I stood in a ring in Germany on top of the boxing world.

I had just defeated Wladimir Klitschko, a man who had reigned for ten years and was the big favourite to defeat me, but I rose to the challenge and triumphed. On the biggest stage possible I gave glory to my Lord and Saviour Jesus Christ, and that immediately divided opinions of me. Then when I returned home, I received widespread criticism in the media and, at the same time, I had already started to drown in depression. This moment of glory quickly turned to dust and it came to the point where I just wanted to die. That's where I will start to unfold my story in the opening chapter, because it reveals my inner drive to be the best heavyweight in the world, while at the same time battling with my mental health issues.

My journey from top amateur to world heavyweight champion hasn't been all dark, and anyone who knows me is aware that I enjoy a laugh as much as the next man. Finding my way out of the darkest of days, I am now back at the boxing summit with the potential to earn more money than I have ever done. Most importantly, I love the life of being a dad, a husband and a brother.

I've developed a new perspective on the boxing business and life in general. I enjoy nothing more than having fun with friends and family, with my fans, and even winding up some of my fellow fighters like Anthony Joshua, the big spaghetti hoop Deontay Wilder, and Wladimir Klitschko, who hated it when I enjoyed imitating him as that film character Borat. Joshua got a surprise when I called him up and said, 'What's happening, AJ? How are you, mush?' And then told him I was going to knock him out and we had a bit of banter. I've got a lot of famous people in my phone's contacts so I can have a bit of fun after I've had a few beers.

In this book I've tried to share the light with the dark. We start with a day in 2010 that would unknowingly change the course of my life – in and out of the ring, for the good and for the bad. From there I relive my upbringing. I share the amazing strength of my loved ones who have stood by me, in my triumphs and in my weakest moments. I chart my journey as the Gypsy King: from amateur to heavyweight champion, from the rise to the fall to the rise again. I want this book to show the real me, warts and all. But above all, and if I only want this book to do one thing, it is to inspire anyone else out there going through a tough time. If I can ask for help about mental health – the 6 foot 9 heavyweight champion of the world – so can you. If I can lose over 10 stone in weight, so can you. Happiness is not found in the things you have. We're all told to get a better job, to get a bigger house, a faster car and we'll feel so much better, and life will be great, but that's just a lie. You can have all of that and still feel worthless.

But there's a way out from the trap of depression, and

I believe that knowing this can give hope to others across the world who are suffering in silence from mental health issues. I just feel that there are too many men and women without a voice, without easy access to explain their fears, or unable to describe what they have to go through on a daily basis just to get by in life. The opportunity to open up about our inner demons can make such a difference.

I was a shy, quiet character growing up and just like a lot of kids in sport I used to get nervous when I was starting out in my amateur days. I had a fear of losing as an amateur because I wanted to succeed so badly. But then when I started professional boxing I thought that if I was going to get attention I had to shout my mouth off, because being myself wouldn't work. So I started playing this part when the cameras would roll, being arrogant and cocky. This mask would go on and I eventually lost myself in this character, because it was what people expected of me, and I suppose that can happen in all walks of life. You can feel like you have to try and be something you're not because of the pressure society puts on you. And this is a big factor in the development of mental health problems. I've realised that I have to be me, no matter what.

I've had to get behind the mask.

CHAPTER ONE

KING FOR A DAY

In June 2010 I boarded a plane for a trip that was longer than I had anticipated and, unknown to me at the time, would set me on the path to defeating Wladimir Klitschko, one of the most dominant world heavyweight champions in the history of boxing. It was also the start of a journey that would derail my life in the most torturous way.

At this point in my career I had lifted my first professional belt, the English heavyweight title. At home I had become a father to our first child, Venezuela, who was a year old. In and outside the ring, things were relatively good because I was fighting regularly and starting to make a name for myself, although my personal demons were never far away.

My personality has always been one of acting instinctively. If I feel I need to do something, I do it. So one day I walked into a travel agent and booked a flight from Manchester airport. Detroit was my destination and the man I was going to see was the late, legendary boxing trainer Emanuel Steward – Manny as he is known. His list of fighters matches any of the great boxing coaches down through the decades. He trained a total of forty-one world champions, including legends of the ring Thomas Hearns, Lennox Lewis and the man who was always my number one target, the long-time undisputed heavyweight champion of the world, Ukrainian Wladimir Klitschko.

Manny was a good amateur boxer – he had a record of ninety-four wins and only three defeats, and he won a national Golden Gloves title in 1963 – but it was as a trainer at the famous old Kronk gym in Detroit that he shone so brightly. His legendary status was long set in stone by the time he took an interest in me, looking across the pond and eager to have a chat. Manny had actually called my dad, John, a year earlier, in 2009, expressing his desire that I come over and see him because he believed that I could be the next heavyweight champion of the world.

That was a very bold statement, and the invitation was naturally very tempting, but I said no because the time wasn't right. My wife, Paris, was pregnant with Venezuela and it just didn't suit me to make such a huge move, even though I felt honoured and excited by the fact that Manny Steward was wanting to meet me, a twenty-two-year-old unbeaten but raw professional. However, one day I just thought, if I don't go to Detroit and see him I'll regret it for the rest of my life, so somehow I had to make it happen. This wasn't just any old trainer wanting to work with me, it was a legend of the sport. So

I booked the flight, grabbed a bag and told Paris I was off to the States. That's the way I am, I have that impulsive nature.

I did try to contact Manny on the phone, as well as my cousin, Andy Lee, from Limerick, who was there training in his gym. But I couldn't get hold of either of them. Manny was very busy with his television commentary work with American channel HBO. So I just got on the plane, on my own with no address for him, and when I arrived at Detroit airport I told the taxi driver to take me to the Kronk gym. When we arrived at what we believed was the gym, the place had closed down, but fortunately the driver found the right address and we eventually got there.

When I walked in I was the only white guy in the place, and standing so tall I stood out a bit. I went up to one of the trainers and asked, 'Where can I find Manny?' He asked me who I was and I told him, 'I'm Tyson Fury, the future heavyweight champion of the world.' When it came to boxing and what I could do in the ring I never lacked confidence. So, the guy rings Manny and says, 'There's a crazy white kid down here says he wants to meet you, says he's going to be the next heavyweight champ of the world.' Manny asked him what my name was, and then he got the guy to bring me straight to his house. He was as shocked to see me as the whole gym was when they saw this big heavyweight with the funny

English accent talking a big game. It's a funny thing, but I was so confident in my ability and yet away from that arena I could find myself being happy one minute and the next slipping into a very dark place. It just felt like the bigger the high, the deeper the low. That was the cycle I was in, so with every bit of success there would be a price to pay. This was my life and I didn't know why.

As soon as Manny and I met we clicked. I was supposed to be there for two weeks and I stayed for a month. He took me back to his house and I stayed there with him; he even bought me a special extra-large bed to sleep in. He treated me and talked to me like I was a world champion already and told me I was one of the top three personalities he'd ever seen in boxing – Muhammad Ali and Prince Naseem Hamed being the other two. He worked a lot on my balance and my jab and in those four weeks I was like a sponge soaking everything in. What he taught me has stayed with me for the rest of my career. He wasn't just a boxing trainer, he was a real teacher and you don't get many of them today. He took an interest in me personally and was keen to pass on as much knowledge as possible about the art of boxing.

It was without doubt one of the best times of my life, particularly with my cousin Andy there as well. He had been with Manny from the start of his professional career and would go on to become WBO middleweight champion. We'd go out with Manny to these bars at the weekend and Manny – who everybody in Detroit knew – would stand up and introduce me as the next heavyweight champion of the world. I'd then grab the microphone and give them a few songs and the Americans loved it.

In the Kronk gym I quickly made an impression. This big Australian cruiserweight kept asking me to spar with him and Manny told him no, because I was too big, but the guy insisted. When we finally did get in the ring I put him down with a jab twice and we had to end the spar shortly after that because it was so one-sided. I was on fire and so was Andy in sparring, and one day all you could hear from one of the veteran trainers was, 'Man, I can't believe it. White boys taking over Kronk! White boys taking over Kronk!'

The way I moved, the rhythm I had and the way I handled myself, the experienced trainers in the gym were really surprised because they viewed most European heavyweights as quite robotic in the way they boxed. The big men in the sport don't normally move the way I do. I stand out because of my movement and hand-speed. Like a diamond in the rough, and they couldn't take their eyes off me. They had expected me to walk in flat-footed, hands held high, marching forward, just another big people-carrier off the conveyor belt, but instead they were looking at a Ferrari.

The old men in the gym said I was boxing more like an American — with an American's mentality. I was backing up the claim I made when I arrived at the gym that I was the future of boxing. I could see that the guys who had been around the gym with Manny for a long time were shocked at what they were witnessing because very few heavyweights can do what I can in the ring, with my natural athleticism and fast hands. They were loving watching me every day and I could sense just how beneficial the whole experience was and the positivity from experienced boxing men was palpable. There was no sense of anxiety, no opportunity for the darkness to descend on my mind because I was learning more about the sport I had always loved, learning from the best and feeding off the reactions of those watching me.

I was really tempted to stay there. I was in one of the most famous boxing gyms in the world and every day catching the eye, putting on a show and then going out to the local bars and entertaining the fellas with my singing in the evenings. I was improving so much. In terms of my development it may have made sense to stay, but I had to get back home to Paris and the family because they were always my number one priority. Manny loved working with me and he actually bought me a pair of beautiful boxing boots, which I would go on to wear the momentous night of my heavyweight title match five years later in Germany.

After a great experience I had to say goodbye to Manny and the Kronk gym. However, four weeks later, I got a call from Manny asking me to come to Austria to be part of Wladimir Klitschko's training camp for his world heavyweight title defence against Londoner Dereck Chisora. I jumped at the chance to be part of that camp – to see what Klitschko was like up close and personal and to have the opportunity of working with Manny again. What I didn't know when I accepted the offer was how Manny was about to lay even more groundwork for me to one day triumph over Klitschko.

We were in the gym one session and Manny pointed to me and said it loud and clear – 'Tyson is going to become the next dominant heavyweight champion of the world.' Wladimir didn't like it one bit and I could see it in his face. He was in the ring sparring and having a tough time, and Manny said, 'I better not let Tyson Fury in here cos he'd knock your ass out.' Manny actually called me at 3 a.m. after that sparring session to ask my thoughts on how Wladimir was looking because he valued my opinion on fighters. I was very honest and told him I went to Austria expecting to meet Superman but he just looked like another man with a pair of gloves on; there was nothing special to see at all. Clearly, Manny was worried that Klitschko was going to pull out of the fight with Chisora because he wasn't looking that sharp at all. In the end, that's exactly what happened, but it wasn't before I got into Klitschko's head even more.

About twenty of us (and my cousin Andy can verify this) went down to the sauna and an old American trainer who worked with Wladimir said to me, 'You know Wladimir is the Sauna King, so show some respect. He likes to leave last after everybody else has gone.'

Well, that was music to my ears because nobody loves a challenge more than me and I knew it was a perfect moment to wind up big Wlad. So we go in, I'm as fat as a pig and it's the hottest sauna that I've ever experienced, with a big fire in the middle of it. We're all there naked and they give you this stuff that looks like chocolate sauce to pour over yourself. One by one they all get out, to the point where it's just me and Wladimir sitting there. We were only meant to be in there for twenty minutes but then he gets up and turns the clock back to go for another twenty minutes and I'm thinking, 'I'm going to die here.' But I wasn't going to let him beat me. I thought, 'If I pass out, they can throw some water on me and I'll be all right.' So I count down the time in my head to keep me focused and then five minutes later Wladimir gets up and walks out in a huff. I thought, great, and stayed in for another ten minutes and when I came out I nearly fainted. The old American trainer who I had spoken to before I went in was still there and he said to me, 'What did you say to Wladimir?' I just looked at him, took in a gulp of air and said, 'Now I'm the Sauna King.'

That's how I knew I would beat Wladimir; he knew that I wouldn't give in to him. Throughout all his camps he would stare at sparring partners, looking to intimidate them. He was big into psychology because he knew there was a good chance that down the line he would face those guys and they would be beaten before the first bell would ring because they would have demons in their head from what had happened in the training camps with him. But he couldn't do that to me. He would stare at me in the gym and I'd shout across, 'Have you got a problem?'

I could see that his weakness was that he needed to be in control of everything. We both left that camp knowing he couldn't intimidate me. And we both knew the same thing five years later when the moment finally came to fight for his world titles at the Esprit Arena in Düsseldorf in 2015.

· · ·

It had seemed a long way off, but Klitschko was always the target for me. As I built up my career, winning every title I could – the English, Irish, British, Commonwealth, European and WBO Intercontinental heavyweight titles – I improved my world ranking in pursuit of big Wlad. He was knocking off one challenger after another and his brother Vitali was doing the same. Vitali first won the WBC belt in 2004 and then held it from 2008 to 2013, while Wlad had the other major three belts, the WBA, IBF and WBO. They had the heavyweight scene wrapped up and it was going to take the Gypsy King to bring down their empire. They knew it and they kept me away from the crown jewels for as long as they could, until I made it to the position of mandatory challenger and my chance came in 2015.

But as my professional career was in the ascendancy and as I approached the biggest fight of my life, there was tragedy at home that had to be suppressed until I fulfilled my dream. The nightmare could come later.

My uncle Hughie, who had coached me in the early part of my career, died in October 2014 after a freak accident. He was moving a caravan when the drawbar fell on him and broke his leg. He then suffered a clot, which travelled to his lung and he suffered a cardiac arrest. He lay in a coma for eleven weeks after the accident and during the early part of that period I found myself not only visiting him in hospital but also having to rush my wife Paris into the same hospital, Wythenshawe in Manchester. Paris was around six months pregnant at the time and we had received the heart-breaking news that the baby had died. Because the little one was so developed, Paris had to go into hospital to have the baby delivered.

Words cannot describe how terrible a time it was for everyone in the family. I was in one part of the hospital with Paris as she had to give birth to our child who had died, and in another ward Uncle Hughie was in an induced coma. I went from one side of the hospital to the other, just to check on my uncle and then back to Paris, who was thankfully allowed home that day.

The hospital wanted to take the baby off us but I told them emphatically no, because that was not in our culture, and that I would be taking him home to bury him. I put him in this little wooden box that I had for a watch, took him up to my dad's house, and found a nice spot in the garden and buried him there. My dad and my brother Shane were with me. Paris naturally didn't go because it was all just so traumatic for her. The tears were streaming down my face as we said a few prayers and I laid down a stone to mark his burial place. It was one of the hardest things I've ever had to do. It really cut me up and yet at the same time I had to be strong for Paris and think about what was best for her because she was in such a state, as any mother would be at having lost a baby in that way.

I was supposed to have a fight in July but that was cancelled and to help Paris cope with the whole trauma she had been through I booked us a cruise. We flew to Venice and spent two weeks on a Mediterranean cruise with Shane and his wife, as well as my very good friend Dave Reay and his wife. I just felt it would help but at first Paris was adamant that she didn't want to go; she was crying a lot and just in despair really. But I managed to persuade her, and while she may not have been in the best form understandably, I think that as the cruise went on it did help her in some way to deal with the grief. It wasn't the first time we had lost a child, and even more tragically it would not be the last, but it was the most traumatic.

I had to continue my career, and my quest to face Klitschko, and the only way I could deal with the loss of the baby and of my uncle Hughie was to bottle it all up. I had no time to grieve; all that trauma had to be put to the back of my mind – as if it hadn't happened – so I could pursue my dream of becoming world champion. It may sound harsh, but it was the only way I could cope and keep my boxing career on the right path.

. . .

At the first press conference to officially announce the fight, which was in Germany, I again made it clear that Klitschko wasn't going to control me the way he had done with all his other opponents. In the second press conference in England, I stole all the limelight when I turned up in a Batman costume, and even staged a fight with the Joker! I had the room in stitches and on my side. But even in the little things, like when we were getting the photographs taken, Klitschko would be trying to tell me to look this way and that. I just said, 'I'll look where I want. I'm beating you and you know it.'

Manny had sadly passed away in 2012 but his words were still in Wladimir's mind. He took everything Manny said as gospel and I knew that. Manny's coaching protégé, Johnathon Banks, was now Wladimir's trainer so the Kronk influence was still there as we prepared to face each other.

Psychologically, I knew that I had him, I knew he was unsure of what to expect from me. But I had to be in top physical shape otherwise I had no chance. After all, I was going in against a man who was undefeated in eleven years and had successfully made eighteen world title defences. To the rest of the world I was turning up to be the latest victim at the hands of Dr Steelhammer, as he was known. Virtually nobody outside of my family and team gave me a chance; they just thought Wladimir was a league above me. The vast majority of media, boxing pundits and former champions didn't give me a hope of being victorious against Klitschko, who at that point had a record of sixty-four wins, three defeats and fifty-three knockouts.

I had beaten some very tough guys along the way to securing that shot at Klitschko. I had proven myself worthy of this opportunity, with an unbeaten record of twenty-four fights and eighteen knockouts, and yet the bookmakers said I was a 4/1 underdog. The general consensus was probably summed up by former world heavyweight champion David Haye, who told the *Guardian* newspaper, 'The best guy on Fury's record is Dereck Chisora, you look at Klitschko and it is a whole different story. This is Tyson's first introduction to world heavyweight boxing. He has never fought anyone who is a true world-class fighter. To go from fighting the Chisoras of this world to go in with a strong, healthy dominant world champion, will be a step too far.'

The funny thing is, maybe if Wladimir had not got injured in training, which led to the fight being postponed for four weeks, all those so-called experts could have been right. Instead of meeting him in October, the new date for my moment of truth would be 28 November 2015.

I had a brutal training camp for the biggest fight of my life. I went into the start of it very unfit. I lost seven stone in eight weeks at our camp in Cannes, France. As usual I had ballooned up between fights. It was a vicious cycle back then that I couldn't get away from; when I wasn't fighting for a long period I would get down and eat too much.

In the build-up to the fight we were training in 33 degrees of heat and to be honest I wasn't sharp at all. I was feeling drained because of the amount of weight that I had lost and my chances for the fight didn't look good. But then word came through that Wladimir had asked for a postponement because of injury and I have to admit that I was relieved. Those four weeks gave me the time to get my energy back, put on a little bit of weight and just get into the shape I needed to be in for fight night. Everything was transformed in that time; it was great for me and bad news for Wladimir.

But despite all the work I had done, and the impact that Manny Steward had on both of us, I will always maintain that I didn't win the fight against Wladimir, God won it for me. He intervened in so many ways. I don't believe anything happens by chance when you trust God; this was the plan he had for me and he had put everything in place for me to triumph. Nothing was going to stop me from being victorious on that amazing night – not even my recent traumas that were still weighing heavily on me throughout training.

When we came together in Düsseldorf for the first official announcement for the new fight date, I made it clear to Klitschko that the young lion had come to finally end the stale, dull reign of the old king. 'You've got about as much charisma as my underpants,' I told him. 'I'm going to rid boxing of your boring jab-and-grab style.'

There were further media commitments before I then

continued my training. The next time we met was during fight week. I kept up the mind games, defiantly telling Klitschko that my moment had arrived – the moment that the great Manny Steward had foreseen.

For me it was extra special that my dad John was able to be at the fight. He had come out of jail in February but still wasn't allowed out of the country at that point. However, after applying to his probation officer, they granted him a visa to attend the fight, which was such a relief both to him and to me. He made it clear to the media and everyone else just how much this moment was going to mean to him. 'I'm not long out of jail. It was a long sentence and all I want to do is see my son be victorious here. If I die on Sunday, I'll die happy because I will have seen what I need to see,' Dad said during fight week. And then he had his own special moment, an unusual spiritual experience just twenty-four hours before I faced Klitschko.

Dad would admit to me later that he was feeling super-stressed about the fight and what might go wrong, so much so that he genuinely felt like he was going to have a heart attack. The dark side of boxing, the politics and the behind-the-scenes antics have ruined the dreams of many boxers and he felt that the power of the Klitschkos within the sport meant that somehow I would be denied the chance to realise my dream. It meant so much to my dad that I would be given a fair opportunity to prove I was the better man.

He was sitting on his bed in his hotel room looking through the blinds in a cold sweat fearing the worst. All of a sudden he could see this light coming through and it illuminated a small cross among the buildings in the distance. He said he just felt all the stress and doubts drain away. He felt transformed; the negative feelings were replaced by positivity, he felt relieved and contented, and he immediately jumped up and came up to my room to see how I was coping. It was the day before the biggest fight of my life but, to his surprise, he opened the door and saw me and my brother Shane dancing and singing on the microphone! I told him I had never felt better and he just told me, 'You can't lose. You're going to be heavyweight champion of the world,' and he closed the door, leaving us to our *X-Factor* rehearsals! I can't imagine Klitschko was that relaxed that night, and he was the champion.

But there was some more stress to go through before that could happen. On the Saturday afternoon I asked to go down to the stadium to check out the ring. After shadow boxing I got out and told my team that I couldn't box on that, it was too spongy. My footwork was going to be crucial if I was going to beat Klitschko so I needed a normal canvas that could allow me to move well – and this wasn't it. I would have been gassed after six rounds because it would have been like boxing on sand. This was the kind of canvas that Klitschko liked; this was the kind that he trained on because he liked to methodically move around the ring. When my uncle and coach Peter checked the canvas there was six inches of thick foam underneath it; it was ridiculous.

And then everything kicked off between my camp, the Klitschkos, the German boxing federation and the World Boxing Organisation officials. It was a screaming match. They were refusing to change the canvas so at around three o'clock in the afternoon, just seven hours before I was due to fight, we gave them an ultimatum: change it within the hour or there's no fight. It wasn't an empty threat. We were ready to get the next flight home because this was just typical of the way the Klitschkos wanted to control every detail.

The official representing the British Boxing Board of Control agreed that the canvas would not have been passed in the UK but the Klitschko team were digging their heels in until it came to crunch time and it was Wladimir's brother Vitali who said, 'Right, just change it.' So, from being minutes away from heading home, I was now once again having to prepare to win the world heavyweight title – and once again we hadn't backed down to the Klitschkos like others had in the past.

We had taken every precaution leading up to the

fight. We brought in our own chef even though we were staying in a good hotel, we had bought water from a supermarket five miles down the road, and even after the fight I refused to drink any water until we were back at the hotel. That might seem extreme but funny things happen in boxing. It was better to be safe than sorry and I had even been warned before I went to Germany to watch out for any tricks.

I had been at a boxing show a few months earlier in England, and the next morning I was having breakfast with my friend Dave Reay when this German boxing official came over to the table. He told us to be very careful about what could happen when we were in Germany. He warned us that our water could potentially be spiked and that even the towels left for us in the dressing room could be laced with something. I was obviously shocked, but forewarned is forearmed. So from that moment onwards Dave knew that his job when flying to Düsseldorf in fight week was to bring water and towels for the day of the fight. Paris was going to fly out but when she learned that Dave and his wife Catherine were also coming, she decided to travel with them by car, bringing the towels along with them.

In the changing room before the fight I remained calm, as I usually do before bouts. Then suddenly I was standing in the tunnel waiting for my name to be announced by the great boxing MC, Michael Buffer. All I could see was flashing lights everywhere and all I could hear was 55,000 people screaming in anticipation of another big Klitschko fight in Germany, a country where he had become an icon. I thought to myself, 'Right, it's all down to me now. I'm not the biggest knockout puncher in the world and I'm up against Mr Defensive Boxer, a champion who has reigned for a decade.'

The enormity of the challenge was real. Klitschko didn't lose in Germany, that was the theory most people in boxing seemed to believe in. He was too powerful. I needed a miracle, but I knew that God was never going to forsake me. It wasn't just about boxing that night. I had a duty to fulfil, a duty to speak about the Lord Jesus Christ, who had brought me to this point against the odds, and I walked into the ring to the song 'I'm Going to Have a Little Talk With Jesus', by Randy Travis. This was my time, the stage I was always meant to be on.

• • •

From the moment I stepped through the ropes I was calm and focused, ready to do my job, to fulfil my mission. I showed my class from the start as I used my jab to great effect. I could see that Klitschko was feeling frustrated because he couldn't get settled to throw his trademark big right hand. He was used to dominating opponents, dictating to them how the fight was going to go but he hadn't faced anyone like me before. I was as big and as strong as he was and had better footwork and more fluid boxing skills. And I was bringing all of that to him from the start. I was outboxing him and I could feel his frustration building and building. I was feeling so confident that even as early as the third round I stuck my hands behind my back and skipped away from his punches.

Everything was going to plan. I was scoring with good single blows and nullifying his work with ease in the first half of the fight. By the end of the sixth round – the halfway point – I felt I had probably won every round and most at ringside seemed to feel the same. The shots I was landing were starting to have an effect on Klitschko's features as he developed a bad cut over his right eye. Some of the later rounds were a little closer but I still felt in command. I was using my feet so well that it was no wonder his team had wanted a thicker canvas to slow me down, because my movement and switch-hitting from orthodox to the southpaw stance was giving him all kinds of trouble. It was something that he had never faced before against a string of previous opponents who were cumbersome by comparison. At times it was a scrappy fight because of the way our styles clashed but there was no getting away from the fact that as the rounds clicked by I was the boss in the ring. The young lion was roaring and Klitschko knew it.

Of course, in a big fight you are never quite sure how the judges are scoring it but that's not in your hands. The only real issue for me was when the referee deducted me a point in the eleventh round for hitting him behind the head, which I thought was a bit unfair. In professional boxing if you win a round it's scored 10–9, unless there is a knockdown and then it will usually be 10–8. The deduction of the point meant the scores could be tightened up. In the final round he caught me with a really good left hook and then a right hand but I took them very well and raised my hands in triumph at the sound of the final bell.

Before the decision was announced I said to myself, 'Please, Lord Jesus, don't let me be robbed in this foreign country tonight,' because I knew that Klitschko was such a big name in Germany that the judges could naturally be influenced by the desire of 55,000 mostly Germans in the arena to see him triumph once again, as they scored the rounds. But when Michael Buffer announced, 'From the United Kingdom, the new unified champion of the world – Tyson Fury!' I jumped into the air in celebration and my dad nearly collapsed because we didn't expect to get a decision in Germany, where Klitschko had seemed to the world unbeatable.

When I was interviewed in the ring I right away said, 'This glory is not for me. This was down to my rock and my salvation, Jesus Christ. He won here tonight.' I heard later that when they showed the fight in delayed coverage in some other countries they cut that bit out. But I had to tell the world that it was my belief in Jesus Christ that enabled me to win the world heavyweight title, to create the biggest upset in heavyweight boxing since Mike Tyson had lost to James Buster Douglas in 1990. In every interview straight after, no matter what the question was, I just told the reporters, 'Believe in the Lord Jesus Christ and you will be saved,' because I knew His power got me through.

Everyone was so excited. My family and friends were just so pleased to see me fulfil my dream. Paris was at ringside in tears and then she came into the ring. Doing the interview with HBO, I broke down in tears for the first time ever in the ring when I described how much it meant to me and dedicated the victory to my late uncle Hughie, who had coached me at the start of my career.

Former world heavyweight champion Lennox Lewis was part of the commentary team for HBO and he was in the ring as well. For a brief moment the former kingpin of the division became my roadie! I handed him my bottle of water as I took his microphone and thanked Klitschko for the chance to fight for the title before singing to Paris, who by this stage was standing beside me in the ring. Off I went with Aerosmith's 'I Don't Want to Miss a Thing' for a full two minutes as the fans lapped it up and the tears streamed down Paris's face. It was an incredible feeling. Those moments in the ring after the verdict had been announced were so joyous, so emotional, they can hardly be placed into words.

Commentating for BBC radio, former world champion and highly respected analyst Richie Woodhall – one of the few who predicted I would win – said: 'I had it by three rounds; there was only one winner. If they had robbed him it would have been a travesty, he boxed sensationally and went to another level. The body language said it all. Wladimir and his brother Vitali knew they did not do enough. I think it's the greatest night of boxing I've ever commentated on. My hat goes off to him. He excelled in every department tonight and deserves to be heavyweight champion of the world.'

I could see how much it meant to all my family and close friends, who knew that I had predicted all along that I would dethrone Klitschko. I remember one night at Dave Reay's house about five years earlier, we were sitting watching one of Klitschko's fights and I turned to Dave and said, 'I can beat him easy, no doubt about it,' and the dream had come true.

I was walking on air as I went back to my dressing room. I had achieved what I always said I would from when I was a little boy hitting my dad's hands. I was on top of the world, the king of boxing. But as we drove back to the hotel my dad said to me, 'This is where the fun and games will start. Prepare for a rocky road; prepare for a storm.'

He felt that me winning the world title would be too much for those with power in the media and the boxing world to handle and sadly he would be proved right. Less than two weeks later I was stripped of the IBF belt and, on arriving home, I walked into a tsunami of criticism. But there was something else, something even more insidious at work, gnawing away inside of me. Even before I had left the arena in Germany, and despite having just experienced the greatest moment of triumph in my life, I started to feel empty. Not physically empty, but emotionally drained. I had reached the pinnacle of my career. Where would I go now? That night I also remember vividly the trauma of the previous few years suddenly hitting me – it was like a delayed reaction catching up. The loss of my uncle Hughie, the pain of burying my little one. That evening the hollow feeling I felt inside – that climbing to the summit of world boxing didn't mean all that much after all – was too much. I knew I was starting to sink into my dark thoughts. What I didn't realise at the time was how deep my despair could be, and how much further I had to fall. My depression was drawing me in inevitably, like a black hole.

. . .

Looking back on that moment today, thankfully I feel differently. On that night I captured the biggest prize in sport against one of boxing's legendary champions. Tyson Fury, undisputed heavyweight champion of the world. For all the pain I've suffered since then, and the torturous road back to recovery, that title success and that special night in Düsseldorf when I shocked the world can never be taken away from me.

We'll return at the end of this book to the build-up and the aftermath of the Klitschko fight, and the extent to which I soared and then fell from grace. But the highs and lows of my character have always been in me, even from childhood. So let us now go back to the very beginning, to where it all began. Let us embark on the journey of the Gypsy King.

CHAPTER TWO

DESTINY'S CHILD

I don't know where it came from, it was just always there – the belief that I would become heavyweight champion of the world. But I wasn't the first person to say it, that was my dad John when I was only a few minutes old – and that was after I had died three times.

My mother Amber has suffered a lot of trauma in her life and I gave her another real fright when I came into the world three months premature. In total she had sixteen pregnancies and only four survived. There's my older brother John, me, then Shane and the youngest of the four boys, Hughie. We also had a sister, Ramona, who was born two days before Christmas 1997 but died two days later, when I was just nine.

Mum has never been to any of my fights, amateur or professional, just because like a lot of mothers she doesn't want to see her son in the ring getting punched. She's a lovely person, a kind-hearted lady who always provided for us and I wouldn't be the man I am today if it wasn't for her. Mum was always there to encourage me. Myself and Shane spent a lot of time with her growing up – more so than with my dad, who was out working from early in the morning to late at night, mainly as a car dealer. But later, when I started boxing, he would be there every step of the way.

Some of my mother's family, who like my dad's side are from the Travellers community, are from a place just outside Belfast, called Nutts Corner, although my mum has family in Wales as well. Years later, in 2011, when I was looking to prove my Irish ancestry so I could fight for the Irish heavyweight title, by chance I actually got to meet some of my mum's family in Nutts Corner. I had flown into Belfast ahead of a fight I was set to have in that great city. I have always found the Irish people very welcoming towards me, and I happened to mention to a friend the name of my old uncle Chasey Price, someone I'd heard my parents talk about. It turns out my mate knew Chasey through trading with him, so we went and had a cup of tea on his farm. It was a day that I will treasure, but it was strange sitting with my uncle and yet still having to battle to prove my Irish heritage.

It was even stranger because both sides of my family have had famous fighting men from Ireland going back over 200 years. I am the latest and most successful in the ring, while the majority of the men who went before me were bare-knuckle fighters. My mother is the daughter of a bare-knuckle fighter, a former King of the Gypsies, while on my father's side of the family I am a distant cousin of

Bartley Gorman, who was the bare-knuckle Gypsy King from 1972 to 1992, and died in 2002. It's no exaggeration to say that Bartley was one of the toughest men who ever lived, and certainly the greatest bare-knuckle fighter in living memory. With his flaming red hair and stocky physique, he described himself as 'the most dangerous unarmed man on the planet', and I wouldn't disagree. He would fight any man, anywhere. He once fought a man down a coal mine, illuminated by the glare of the miners' lamps. He fought at racecourses, in campsites, even in a quarry. And he never lost. Not once in twenty-five years. He once said, 'I will never fight a normal man . . . I'm liable to kill him with one punch.'

Bartley had apparently been inspired to start fighting when he saw a fighter kill his own uncle with one punch when he was just nine years old. Bartley would live until the age of fifty-seven, when he sadly met his maker at the hands of liver cancer. But hundreds of Travellers attended his funeral and his legacy lives on, particularly in his adopted home of Uttoxeter, Staffordshire, where there is a monument to him. Someone told me that in the Batman film *The Dark Knight Rises*, Tom Hardy even used Bartley's voice as inspiration for his character Bane. He must have had some presence.

But the tradition in my family of fighting men actually goes back even further, to another famous man within the

Travellers community who had the same name, the original Boxing Bartley Gorman. My great-great-great-grandfather Bartley Gorman, the first of his name, was a tough Irish bare-knuckle champion in the nineteenth century who fought all over Mayo. His talent and success started the fighting line. Following on from him there was my great-uncle Ticker Gorman, who fought throughout the 1920s and into the 1940s. His mother and father had come to live in England. He was 6 foot 2 and 14 stone and could really fight. So much so, he would spar with professional boxers such as the great Len Harvey, who won British titles at middleweight, light-heavyweight and heavyweight between 1929 and 1939. He also sparred with Canada's former Commonwealth heavyweight champion Larry Gains, who ended up as a sergeant major in the British Army during the war and was beaten twice by Harvey in title fights. Ticker loved fighting that much he was still taking men on at fairground booths well into his sixties. My dad's grandmother was a Gorman and she married a man called Peter Fury. Those men fought for pride and honour across the UK and Ireland. The fighting spirit inside them flows down through the generations to this day.

I've carried on that fighting heritage as has my heavyweight cousin Hughie, son of my former trainer Peter, and my cousin Hosea Burton, who lost his British light-heavyweight title in December 2016 and told me afterwards that he would rather have died and won than gone home to his family having lost – that's what the fighting honour means.

The title of King of the Gypsies has always been a big deal within the Travellers community down through the centuries. My great-grandfather on my mother's side, Othea Burton, had that title, never losing a bare-knuckle fight in his life. He had one famous fight at Puck Fair in Killorglin, Co Kerry in Ireland, which is held to this day every summer. The fight went on for an hour and a half and has entered Travellers folklore, with the strong rumour being that a scene in the great movie *The Quiet Man*, where John Wayne brawls with his brother-in-law across the countryside, was based on that day when Othea Burton was crowned King of the Gypsies.

The art of boxing is very different from the bare-knuckle days, but the grit, honour and natural fighting heart remains the same. My dad knows all about bare-knuckle fighting and has the scars of battle all over his body. In his words, when he fought, from a teenager upwards, it was kill or be killed. It was savage, with biting, head-butts, elbows – anything went, and it only stopped when someone said they were done. Then afterwards the two men would go for a pint because whatever differences they had were now settled. Boxing is completely different; it's more disciplined and a real art. You can't compare the two.

Money comes and goes but honour remains. And it wasn't just the men in the family who could fight either as my grandmother on my dad's side, Patience, was no pushover. In fact, they say she was more aggressive than my grandfather, who was more or less afraid of his own shadow. He sadly suffered from mental health issues and, of course, in those days it wasn't treated seriously.

But my grandmother would have been tough on her sons, my dad John and uncles Peter and Hughie, who would both go on to train me at different stages of my professional career. Patience stood 5 foot 7, with dark brown hair and hazel eyes and took no nonsense from anyone. She made it clear to my dad to always stand up for himself and never back down and if the boys got out of line she would give them a clip around the ear. My dad jokes that she would rather have a fight than her breakfast!

So fighting was in my DNA and from the moment on 12 August 1988 I came out of my mother's womb weighing in at just one pound I was showing my fighting spirit just to stay alive. My mum and dad feared the worst again when I struggled for life and the doctors made it clear that it was a 100/1 shot that I would make it through the night.

But when I opened my eyes after coming back to life for the fourth time, my dad has told me that he looked at me and said, 'He's going to make it, he'll be 7 foot tall, 20 stone, he's going to be called after Mike Tyson and he'll be the heavyweight champion of the world.' I was three months premature and far from out of the woods. I had to stay in the hospital for another three weeks before I could be brought home. But that wasn't the end of me and the hospital; I would end up going back and forth so often for years to come that I should probably have had a loyalty card.

Right up to the age of eight or nine I suffered from boiling temperatures that would make me delusional. I'd be screaming at my mum and dad that lions were going to eat me and that the curtains were on fire. I had to be rushed to hospital so many times in order for them to monitor me and to get my temperature down; it was frightening for me and my parents. We didn't know what was happening to me or when it would stop, and really it just seemed that it was something I had to go through before I grew out of it.

This may seem unbelievable to many now, when they see me on television fighting on some of the biggest stages in the world, or holding court at press conferences, but I was not an overly confident boy, far from it. I was a bit timid and unsure and always anxious. I worried that something was going to go wrong, and I had no idea at the time why I was thinking like that.

But when it came to boxing, just like my feeling of invincibility against Wladimir Klitschko years later, I always had confidence; I was supremely confident in what I could do boxing-wise. Growing up in Styal village, near Manchester, I had a lot fun and enjoyed attending my local primary school, which only comprised a total of thirty-six pupils. I played in goal for the football team because I was bigger than most so I was quite effective, and I even played for a while on the netball team with the girls, which I wasn't too bad at either! That was a great primary school, there was no trouble and I was liked by all the teachers. I was treated with respect and I showed respect, so I enjoyed going there and learning and playing with the rest of the kids.

My environment, the way I grew up, was a lot different to the way my dad John grew up in the Travellers community. When he was young in the 1960s and 70s he suffered a lot of racism and bullying. It became a ritual that at the end of school every day he would be picked on and would have to fight, going home with a black eye, or cuts and bruises, and eating his dinner with blood in his mouth. Nobody at the school cared because in his view those from the Travellers community were just seen as no-good gypsies, who were treated as if they shouldn't even be breathing the same air as the rest of the kids in his class. He would go home and complain to my grandmother Patience, and she would just tell him to fight back or he would have to answer to her too! He had no option but to learn how to handle himself, as did my uncles Peter and Hughie.

. . .

A lot of people in the UK still seem to have a poor attitude towards Travellers and, to be honest, there are some who give the community a bad name. There are those who steal, who scam people and who will move from area to area leaving a mess. But that's a minority and, as with everyone in life, we are all individuals and should be treated that way. Instead, racism towards Travellers is tolerated. It is often mentioned, when looking back at the great career of Muhammad Ali, that he threw his Olympic gold medal from the 1960 Games into a river, after being refused service at a coffee shop in his home town of Louisville, Kentucky. I can relate to that because I've had the experience with my friend Dave Reay of being point-blank refused entry into a pub because I'm a Traveller. That's something that just should not be tolerated in this day and age.

My dad said that he became hardened to his situation; it was just normal to have to live with that kind of racism on a daily basis. His family were moving around every eight weeks from caravan site to caravan site throughout Yorkshire, so he would arrive at different schools and keep having to go through the same torture because he was seen as the outsider and someone who was less well off than the rest of the kids. He did have it tough as a young boy and a teenager. There wasn't much money around and no chance of making friends in that kind of school environment.

I didn't have the same experience because I wasn't brought up in the same rough areas and I never had a fight in school in my whole time there. I enjoyed school; I was part of the community. I suppose it was a different era, and it also helped that the area was a lot different to those my dad had grown up in.

My dad came to Styal when he was twenty-six; he wanted to try and give us a different life. He knew how hard his young days had been and the cruelty that he suffered so he decided there was no way he was going to put his kids through it. He saw a different way of life. He made friends outside the Travellers community who helped him in his business and he gained respect, though sadly he would admit to not having any really close friends. He's a straight-talker and not everybody likes that – as I have found out to my cost as well.

So Dad bought this 200-year-old dilapidated cottage, with no running water or electricity, on quite a large piece of land, and got to work turning it into our home. For a few years we lived in a caravan as he brought in bricklayers, electricians and whoever else he needed to help renovate the cottage. He did all the hod-carrying and labouring and after ten years he had it the way he wanted and we moved in. There was no such thing as a bank loan or mortgage for my dad; he had to earn the money through car dealing and roofing jobs so he could build it bit by bit. Then disaster struck in the mid-1990s when the cottage flooded, and it took another four years before we could move back into it again. But it was a wonderful place to grow up in and my dad still lives there.

. . .

While my time at school was very enjoyable, like the majority of Travellers I left school around ten years of age. A long education is not part of the Travellers community culture. The average boy is encouraged to get out and start doing work before secondary school age and my dad just had the same attitude – that there is a big world out there and if you want some money then you need to go out and earn it.

I was always around my dad as he sold cars and I learned about dealing – making money and losing money. By the time I was twelve or thirteen I had been in and out of every top car, whether that was a Ferrari, Bentley, Porsche; you name it, I had been in it. As a teenager I was buying and selling. I would go to the auctions with my dad, picking up cars. My dad used to have a pitch in Bolton where he would sell cars and I would help out. But from the house I would do my own selling. I would paint and polish up old cars and sell them for a few hundred quid. It was a good, valuable lesson. It taught me to save and appreciate what I earned.

One of the toughest jobs I had was lifting bricks as well as shovelling stones in a car park that had to be levelled. I would be there from eight o'clock in the morning, work until four and then be in the gym for six that same night and not come out until ten o'clock. It was hard, hard work but I was using the labouring as training and it was developing my arms, legs and shoulders. I was getting £20 per pile that I got shifted so I could walk away with £80 a day and I felt great about that. Shane had been offered the job before me but he couldn't stick it – it was too tough for him.

I was a teenager with a dream of becoming the heavyweight champion of the world. I was training, working and reading. I would read *Boxing News* magazine and the Bible. That was my life and all those family experiences, the lessons on life and my family background gave me the grounding to be the person and fighter I am today. My dad and his dad were both great salesmen – my dad could sell sand to the Arabs and ice to the Eskimos, and I have that natural ability as well. I think I've also shown that I can sell myself pretty well when it comes to big fights!

I lost out on a few deals along the way but I was learning, and when I would tell my dad that I had come up short he would just laugh because, as far as he was concerned, I was learning about life. I may have left school at ten but I was sharp with the numbers and becoming street-smart. And anyway, I was never going to be a doctor or anything like that. I was always going to be a fighter. Some people can be very clever, very academic, but as green as a fresh field, whereas I was at the university of life from a young age. But I do believe that a formal education is very, very important for kids.

The Travellers community, for the most part, hasn't moved on in that regard and I think they need to because for me education can unlock the door to so many opportunities. It can break down barriers and allow people from different parts of society to mix and gain a greater understanding of each other. For me that can only be a good thing if you want society to improve; and for racist thoughts and attitudes to disappear then education is absolutely key to that happening.

The importance of a good family unit is a clear positive within the Travellers community. We see today how the breakdown in family life has badly damaged society, but when it comes to education I think there needs to be a new way of thinking. At the moment the general thought among Travellers is that only idiots go to school, but that's just because they can't see the benefits of a good education, the possibilities that it can open up for young people.

That's certainly what I want for my kids. I want them to have a good childhood, to have strong morals and I'll be encouraging them to go to secondary school and beyond. Maybe we could even have the first Dr Fury one day! I would be very, very proud if one of my children were to be the first to graduate from university and I would even love to have a shot at doing a degree myself.

But for me, having left school, it was time to start earning some money. This meant doing all kinds of jobs, like brushing snow away from driveways for a few quid and then eventually, when I was about thirteen, going out with my brother to collect scrap. I was able to drive by this point and not that far off 6 foot tall. So my brother Shane, my cousin Justin and I would go around the local estates and collect anything that people were throwing out. We'd spend all day at that and then take it to the scrap yard that night and maybe end up with forty or fifty quid.

I often used to think that the way we were living

was something like that popular television programme *The Darling Buds of May*, where the family grew up in the countryside, living life their way. I used to keep a lot of chickens, including some American fighting cocks, about fifty to sixty at a time. I didn't have them for fighting. They were my pets and I would go all over the country, even to Ireland, for shows.

I loved looking after them. It was a bit of an obsession and I remember one day getting up at 5 a.m. and walking twelve miles with my cousin Justin to a market to buy a prized chicken. I was about thirteen and we bought this beautiful chicken; we thought it was a great buy. But for some reason we started arguing on the way home about who would carry it and it got a bit heated. It got to the point when I ended up pushing him away and that led to the chicken flying out of his arms and as it flew up a train was coming and it went smash into the oncoming train. All we had to show for our efforts and money spent on this lovely chicken was a load of feathers blowing over the railway track and a large splat on the front of the train!

· · ·

My brother Shane and I have always been close because we are only a year apart. He has always been around when I've been preparing for fights, and growing up we shared a passion for boxing. But like most brothers we've had our disagreements . . . like the time he came into the garage and tore down all the wood I spent hours stacking under the orders of our dad. I was fuming because it had taken me all day to do it and I knew if Dad came home and saw it wasn't done I was going to be in big trouble. If Dad asked you to do something it was expected to be done, no questions asked. So I just lost my rag with Shane, lifted a big piece of wood and ran after him, giving him such a whack that it knocked out all of his baby teeth. When Dad saw his gaping mouth and the remains of his teeth he knew what had happened, and who had caused it, so needless to say I was the next one getting a good smack!

Growing up, the big passion in my life was always boxing. It was there from a very early age. As soon as I could use a pencil I was drawing pictures of gloves and different boxing kits, colouring in shorts and socks and gloves and then also writing short stories about boxing, describing fights. I'd take them and show my dad and tell him that one day I was going to be a boxer.

My other two brothers, John and Hughie, had some interest in boxing but not the same passion as I had or even Shane for that matter. My dad had fought as a heavyweight in the late 1980s and early 90s, boxing some of the best in Britain, including Henry Akinwande, who went on to win the WBO heavyweight title. But Dad felt used and abused as a professional fighter, believing he never had the chance to truly progress. He never really wanted me to become a fighter because he feared I wouldn't get a fair crack of the whip. He hated the politics of professional boxing and that's why he never encouraged me to be a boxer.

But my dad did get an up-close-and-personal view of my talent when I was just fourteen. He was still keeping in decent shape and was working out on a bag in our shed and we got talking about his career. I cheekily said to him that I'd been watching him on video and he wasn't that good! So he said, 'Right, let's get the gloves and see how you can handle yourself.' He thought he was going to give me a right beating but early on I cracked him with a left hook. Boom! His ribs cracked but he came right back at me. But I was beating him up and we agreed that it was better for him to sit down because I was getting the better of him. In the fourteen fights he had as a professional he admitted to me that he had never been hurt like that. I think we both knew then that I was a bit different and that making a special career for myself in professional boxing was not going to be a problem for me – at least in the ring.

That moment had a big impact on me because I knew how tough my dad was and it just added to my confidence and helped fuel my dreams. In my head I was aiming for the stars but at this point I still hadn't had any proper sparring, a critical part of training and learning how to box. It replicates what you can expect in the ring when fighting for real, only when you spar you have head-guards on. My first real spar came when my dad took me along to Franny Hands' gym in Liverpool, where he always worked out. He told me to sit and behave as he went about his training, hitting the pads and bags as well as doing some sparring. I begged and begged for him to let me spar with an older guy in the gym and finally I was allowed. I got in and poleaxed the guy, who was much more experienced. Franny and my dad couldn't believe it. I was so excited and pumped up that at the end of my first spar I spewed the McDonald's burger and milkshake I'd had on the drive to the gym all over Franny's canvas.

I was now desperate to find an amateur gym to go to. I had no idea about any club nearby but then one day myself and Shane were working in a field for a local farmer, pulling out the ragweed, which is something that can poison horses. Coming towards the end of the day and looking forward to my £10 wages, I got an even better reward when one of the other lads in the field happened to tell me about Jimmy Egan's Boxing Academy, which was only three miles from my home. All the time I'd lived in Styal, near Wilmslow, and I didn't realise that Jimmy's gym was in Wythenshawe, just three miles away. I guess my dad really didn't want me to be a boxer! But this was my chance, I thought, and Shane and I ran home totally pumped because we now knew where we could go to give boxing a real go.

Jimmy ran the gym with his son Steve, and when Shane and I arrived they put us together with the beginners. I was 6 foot 5 and nearly 15 stone at just fourteen so you could say that I stood out a bit. I had never been taught how to fight, it was just in me, and from the moment I was in that gym I knew this was my home; this was where I was always meant to be.

Before I left that first night, Steve had told his dad to get me a medical card – that's the record book that every amateur boxer has. They knew I was a natural and didn't want to let me go. Steve took one look at me and told his dad, 'Heavyweights don't move like that. Get him a card.'

I moved straight into the boxers' class. This was my world; I was never going to do anything else. This was it for me, I thought. Boxing, boxing, boxing . . . I would go to the local car boot sale and buy every boxing video I could and then go home and for hours watch the best fighters who ever lived – Muhammad Ali, Jack Dempsey, Sugar Ray Robinson, Larry Holmes, Sugar Ray Leonard and Mike Tyson, who I watched with special interest because I wanted to live up to his name. I wanted to know everything about the sport because I wanted to join the greats; this was going to be my life.

My first fight was supposed to happen in Bredbury, Greater Manchester, when I was fifteen. About a hundred people had come to see me and I was super-excited, so much so I travelled into Manchester city centre to make sure that I would have tassels on my shorts, just as I had designed as a five-year-old for my dad to see. Mum sowed the tassels on my shorts and boots and I was ready to take my first step on my boxing journey. It was all looking good until we got to the scales and my opponent took one look at me and vanished. My size had scared him off. I was gutted but looking back maybe it was a sign that my road to the top was not going to be straightforward.

I was developing very quickly in the gym with Steve, but so I could get some good sparring my dad would take me to different gyms across England. By the time I was sixteen, I was going to Huddersfield to spar with the British and Commonwealth cruiserweight champion Mark Hobson, who was preparing to fight future world cruiserweight and heavyweight champion David Haye. I did very well and then news started to spread like wildfire about me. We used to go and train in Leicester twice a week and the trainer there, Nick Griffin, said that I would be world champion. I sparred lots of professionals and always felt comfortable. I was on my way.

I eventually had my first fight at RAF Wyton in Cambridgeshire, stopping my opponent Duncan Lee. At the time there were only three junior super-heavyweights active in England and Duncan had already beat the other fella, so when I stopped Duncan I instantly became the best junior super-heavyweight in the country after just one fight. You could say that at RAF Wyton I had lift-off!

Having that first win felt great and the gym was like a second home to me, it was where I had to be. I could be out with Shane somewhere and having a good time with friends but then I would just stop and tell him we had to be at the gym in an hour, and it didn't matter what was happening, I had to be there. I was the first there and last to leave. That might sound strange to some because of the issues I've had with my weight as a professional, piling on the pounds ahead of many camps, but I loved boxing, it came so natural to me and I wanted to see how good I could be so I was going to give it everything.

I was dreaming big. I wanted to be the heavyweight champion of the world, so it was all or nothing. I had found my destiny.

CHAPTER THREE

PARIS

In the Book of Proverbs in the Bible it states, 'a wife of noble character who can find? She is worth more than rubies.' When I reflect on the life I have had with my wife Paris, I am aware just how blessed I am to have her by my side and how blessed our children are to have her as a mother.

Together we have had some magical highs and we have gone through some terrible lows. I have let her down with my behaviour at times and many other women would have walked away. But Paris knows how deep my love is for her and I know how much she loves me, and that is why we have been there for each other. It's why I have been able to come through the worst periods of my life and get myself back on track. Without Paris I don't believe I would still be here.

My amateur career was really just starting to get going when I first met the love of my life in 2005 at a wedding in London. Paris was fifteen and I was seventeen. Right away I felt drawn to her but the feeling didn't seem to be mutual. We were introduced to each other by one of her aunties who was known as a bit of a matchmaker.

Unfortunately, I think Paris thought her auntie had got this one wrong because Paris took one look at me and thought I looked about thirty with my big sideburns and stubble – and by that stage I was huge for my age. It's fair to say, it wasn't the most promising start to a potential relationship. We just said a quick hello and goodbye.

We actually had our first real conversation a year after that wedding when I was invited by a mutual friend to her sixteenth birthday party in Doncaster. It was still just small talk, but this time we hit it off. Because I was quiet and so tall for my age I felt a little weird and would hunch over a bit. But as we were talking it was Paris who told me to straighten up and to walk tall. This small act of kindness made a huge difference to me at the time. If only she had known then. And thanks to her, nowadays she says I stroll around like a proud peacock!

After that first conversation, I knew right away that Paris was the woman for me and every weekend I would travel an hour and a half from Styal in Manchester to Doncaster to see her. I became her first boyfriend and we dated for three years. Then one day I told her that I was going to be a professional fighter, the British champion, and oh, that I was going to marry her.

She thankfully said yes! We got married very young – I was twenty and she was eighteen – and we tied the knot in front of 400 guests at a ceremony in Doncaster.

But Paris's parents were fine with it because they had seen how serious I was about her and how well I treated her. We didn't sleep together until our wedding night. Even after we got engaged, when I would visit her at her parents' home on weekends in between training and fights, I would sleep in a caravan in the yard, while Paris would sleep inside her home on her own. That might seem strange to many in today's western world but that is the tradition of those within the Travellers community and it's also the teaching of the Bible.

Life felt glorious around this time. Paris and I had a lot of fun together and I was loving my boxing. Paris and I have the same values and she is a strong woman; if she feels I'm in the wrong she'll tell me. She's always known the real me, even back then; the man behind the boxer, the man behind the public persona that I would eventually develop. She understands me probably better than anyone else.

Around this time, from the ages of sixteen to twenty, despite so many things going well for me, I was having these anxiety attacks that would come out of nowhere. I didn't understand it was depression yet, because I didn't know what that was. There were some terrible moments, when I'd feel really, really low. I'd feel nothing was worth doing, and I felt worthless. How did I deal with it? I just accepted that I was a moody person – I didn't know what else to think and there was nobody to help me understand it.

I certainly never went anywhere to get help as a young lad because I didn't know I needed to, and my family didn't realise there was such a big issue to address either, because they didn't understand my behaviour at times. This was despite mental health issues having been in my family for generations, and my grandfather suffering from them for most of his life. In fact, he used to be given a tablet, which he thought was for his state of mind but it was actually just a placebo; there was nothing in it but he convinced himself it worked and it helped him to get through the day.

At this time, boxing helped me because when I was focused on boxing, when I had my mind set on something, a goal, a challenge, then I was generally in a good place in those young amateur days. The problems often came when I would go back to everyday reality, periods of inactivity as a fighter, which was something that I would also have to deal with later in my career as a professional fighter. In these periods I could get so low that I would feel suicidal.

At first, and this was many years before my depression was diagnosed, Paris couldn't come to terms with how my mood would change and it would frustrate her. She knew there was something not quite right with me because when we were first dating she would witness how my temperament could change like the flick of a switch. Then after we were married it became more and more obvious just because we were living together. There were times when she would be wondering why I was so upset. I would be at a point when I was constantly in a bad mood and go into a raging temper, screaming and shouting for no reason. There were times when I woke up feeling on top of the world and then feeling the world was on top of me, at times wanting to die every day.

In the Travellers community this kind of thing was not something that was faced up to. The attitude was kind of, 'Shake it off, what's your problem?' In fairness, I think no matter what background people are from, this is often the attitude people going through mental health issues are faced with.

But on many occasions, even when she didn't understand, Paris would be sympathetic. She would try to help me, to listen. She knew it was totally out of character and she did her best to understand. You can't ask for anything more than that from those around you because they are obviously feeling pain just watching the state you're in. Paris would ask me why I was acting the way I was, feeling angry or distant, and I didn't have an answer. At times that made it worse for her and I can understand that. In time she would realise that it wasn't mood swings, it was an illness, and when people recognise it as that then their whole perspective changes.

That's why I think now, looking back, it's so important that parents and partners communicate with their kids and loved ones to get them the medical help they need if the problem is deeper than simply mood swings. You can't stick your head in the sand and expect the problems to go away, or just think a child or a person needs to toughen up, to just give themselves a shake and get on with life.

Years later, when I hit my lowest point, I would put Paris through sheer hell and it almost cost us our marriage. But during my amateur days, the good times mostly ruled over the bad ones. Like my mother, the main thing Paris had to contend with was watching her man step into the ring each time. Boxing is a brutal business and being at ringside for my fights is not something that Paris has ever enjoyed at all. Just like for most partners or parents, it's a nerve-racking experience to see your loved one put their life on the line every time they step through the ropes. From day one in our relationship, Paris hated every second I was in the ring. For the fans I'm an entertainer, but for Paris it's all stress, stress, stress from the first bell to the last and she could do without it. But she has always felt that she's needed to be there for me, to be a support for me, and that has always meant a lot. You can't put a value on that love. Having a happy home is just priceless and to have a rock like Paris in my life means everything. We've proved to each other that together we can face anything.

CHAPTER FOUR

VESTED INTERESTS

I didn't start boxing for the money. As a teenager I walked three miles to Jimmy Egan's gym in Wythenshawe and three miles back almost every day because for me, like every young fighter who puts on their amateur vest, it was about the love of the sport, the challenge. I felt that I was in control, and that the results and the rewards were all down to me. That's how it should be. But then, just like it can happen in professional boxing, there comes a point when as an amateur boxer you realise that politics are at work behind the scenes. I would be no exception when my 2008 Beijing Olympics dream was on the line. That Games would have marked my twentieth birthday and the pinnacle of my amateur career. But it wasn't to be. Instead, it was the culmination of boxing smoke and mirrors that defined much of my amateur career, even though it all began so brightly.

· · ·

By my late teens, getting to the point of being a top senior amateur boxer had come relatively quickly to me, despite my big size meaning I couldn't get enough opponents who wanted to fight me. My amateur trainer Steve Egan at Jimmy's had taken a real interest in me from the start, even if his first impression was down to the fact that I was called Tyson and my surname was Fury. He told me years later that when I had walked into his gym at the age of fourteen and told him my name he thought it was a wind-up. I suppose I can see why, because I can't think of anyone with a name better suited to ring combat than Tyson Fury!

But when he had accepted that I wasn't pulling his chain, Steve got to work with me, and for the next five years he taught me the art of boxing, and that started with a good jab. The importance of the jab in boxing cannot be overestimated. It's the solid, straight shot that – if you're good enough – can almost win you some fights on its own. It didn't take Steve long to see that I was soaking up everything he was teaching me like a sponge. And when it came to the jab it was obvious from the outset that it was going to be a serious weapon for me – and it remains so to this day.

Steve put a lot of hard work into me. He was eager to see how much I could develop, and as we worked together he taught me how to think like a middleweight rather than as a heavyweight. The reason for this, he said, was because he wanted me to be different and a cut above the usual big guys. To do this, Steve made me focus on my speed – good sharp footwork and fast hands, throwing ten- and fifteen-punch combinations in training as well as switching from the orthodox style to the southpaw stance.

In the orthodox style, which is used by most fighters, a boxer leads with their left hand for the straight jab shot, whilst they position their footwork in such a way that their left foot is ahead of their right. This stance typically favours a right-hander's dominant side, allowing them to open up with a bigger shot with their right hand, whilst leaving their 'weaker' left side closer to their opponent. Southpaw is basically the opposite: your right hand leads the jab, with your right foot further forward than your left. This stance is mostly favoured by left-handers who are stronger on that side. My ability to switch between the two stances would give me a competitive advantage, and is a style that I have refined and refined over the years.

I gelled very well with Steve. We had excellent chemistry and it just seemed that everything in boxing was coming naturally to me. I instinctively counter-punched – I worked out very quickly how a guy could come at me, how I could defend, how I could spot and exploit the opening in his guard as a result of his attack, and then I could make him pay instantly with a return punch of my own. If there was something that I needed to work a bit harder on to make me even more effective as a fighter it was 'coming forward' – I was more often the defender than the aggressor in the ring, happier waiting for my opponent to make a mistake than walking him down, looking to land my own big shots first. That took more work but it wasn't a problem for me and I was soon creating angles of attack, slipping and sliding in the ring with ease, which had Steve drooling about how far I could go in my career.

After only two fights, Steve thought about putting a bet on me, that I would one day be heavyweight champion of the world. He'd been expecting to get odds of 10,000/1 but the bookmakers were only offering 250/1, so he didn't bother! But it nevertheless showed the belief he had in my ability at such an early stage. When it came to backing me, Steve was there every step of the way, along with my dad.

However, I soon experienced the murkier side of the fight game. I remember early on in my amateur career, when I was a teenager and it was still very hard to get me matched due to my size, Steve took me down to a fight on the south coast. I was a little nervous but mostly just excited about the bout, and I had been training for weeks. Yet as soon as we got in the ring, to my shock the judges had already filled in my scorecard, recording that I'd lost the fight before a single punch had even been thrown. Steve looked at me and said right away that I wouldn't be fighting that day. I was angry and dejected and threw off my gloves. We stormed out of there and went straight home, so that there would be no loss on my record. I was disappointed not to fight, but the behaviour of the officials was really a total disgrace. We never fully found out why that happened, but I was clearly meant to be a grateful loser.

Back in Jimmy's gym, the work on my development continued and one of the best regular sparring partners I would have in my early years was my brother Shane, to the point that at times he would frustrate me because he knew my boxing style so well. That could get me down a little, but Steve was there to make me realise that nobody knew me better than Shane and that this was just part of my overall development. Sparring in those early years would be a hugely formative experience for me, whether I was on top in the ring or not. I felt at home in that arena and I could showcase my innate fighting heart, because whenever someone would catch me in the ring with a good punch, I immediately wanted to fire back. The more a punch stung me, the more I wanted to retaliate, and with even more spite. I took it as an insult for someone to catch me with a good shot and in many ways I still feel the same way today. I know at times you have to take your punishment and take your medicine, but when I'm in that ring I believe I'm the one with the PhD in the sweet science of boxing; I'm the doctor who should be handing out the medicine every time!

From the age of sixteen, after a few high-profile sparring sessions, word started to spread about me across the country, even though I hadn't fought that much. I sparred with former British heavyweight title challenger Pelé Reid, who was based in Sheffield with the late, great trainer Brendan Ingle, and I dominated him. Brendan was the man behind former world champions Prince Naseem Hamed and Johnny Nelson as well as a host of other major title holders. He always emphasised the art of boxing so when he saw me deploy my wide skillset he was impressed.

One fight that stands out from those early days in the ring was when I was matched with a guy who had the nickname 'Facebreaker'. I don't even remember his actual name, but he was the same size as me, the same age and he had three straight knockout wins on his record. In the bout before we met he hit someone so hard he broke his cheekbone and then knocked the guy clean out, so that's how he got the nickname! A lot of people thought he could be too much for me. But Steve had no doubt that even though I still had a long way to go before I had fully developed physically, I could outbox such a tough guy. Fortunately for me (and my cheekbones), Steve was right. I went in and schooled the Facebreaker; he never landed a punch.

In my fifth bout, I faced a guy called Danny Hughes, who was gaining a big reputation in the north-east of England. I knew it was going to be an even sterner test but that didn't stop me messing about with my brother Shane before we got in the car for the trip to Newcastle. Shane was annoying me and I went to hit him, missed him and hit our wardrobe – and broke the knuckle in my right hand. My hand was swollen and I was in a lot of pain, but there was no way I was backing out of fighting Hughes. I knew that a lot of people thought he was going to be too good for me – I think it's fair to say that has been something of a theme throughout my career. So I made my way up to Newcastle, somehow blagged the medical and then got ready for the first bell.

Everyone – including myself – was in for a massive surprise. Hughes came charging at me looking to land a big punch. I simply stepped back and caught him with a big right hand that knocked him out in just twenty-five seconds. It was a huge win for me; I could see the shock on the faces of all his supporters – and they didn't even know about my broken knuckle. Hughes would go on to become a professional and only lost to good fighters like Audley Harrison, Michael Sprott and my cousin Hughie Fury, but he was never knocked out like he was that night.

That evening after the fight, as you can imagine, my coach, my family and me were all buzzing. There was so much enthusiasm in fact that we left Newcastle and headed home without my younger brother Hughie, who we accidentally left at the hotel, Macaulay Culkin-style! He was left crying his eyes out in the hotel lobby until we remembered and quickly swung the car around. We dried his eyes and got him a McDonald's for the drive home. I hope by today he's forgiven us.

But it wasn't just those around me who were starting to get excited about how far I could go as an amateur. I later found out that Alvin Finch, an international referee, had made a call to the head of the international squad to tell them about what had happened in the Hughes fight. It was after that bout that my trainer Steve got a call about me coming to train with the English squad.

Off the back of this call-up, I was all set to box in the top amateur tournament in the UK, the Junior ABAs (Amateur Boxing Association Championship), but for that year in 2004, they oddly decided to suspend the heavyweight division. I was told that they thought I was too big for everyone else and that I was older than what I was claiming I was – just fifteen years old. I was frustrated that people didn't believe me, but I let my boxing do the talking. I fought in the men's novices' competition instead, for those with ten fights or less under their belt, and I wiped the floor with everybody.

I was loving boxing and I couldn't get enough time in

the gym or the ring. After just seven bouts I won a multi-nations tournament in Dublin, in the process beating the European Union junior champion in the match for gold. I was truly up and running in my career and my confidence was growing and growing with each victory.

I stayed on a roll and after just nine bouts I was selected to represent Great Britain at super-heavyweight in the World Junior Championships in 2006, aged eighteen. I remember the GB coach on the plane to Morocco saying that 'we're taking Tyson for experience; we don't expect him to win anything', which looking back was understandable, but I had other ideas. I never went into any competition or any fight just for experience. With me, it was always about shooting for the very top.

Going to Morocco as a young lad from Manchester was a very humbling experience because everywhere I looked there were signs of great poverty – kids begging on the streets, people with very little going for them. It hit me hard because up to that point in my life I hadn't witnessed anything as extreme as that.

I beat a good guy from Azerbaijan in the first round of the championships and then stopped the Hungarian István Bernát, who went on to have a good senior career. I had secured a bronze medal at the very least but I was feeling confident of going all the way. The semi-final was an exciting, back-and-forth bout against Sardor Abdullaev of Uzbekistan. After the final round I felt – as did my GB coaches – that I was the winner and that I clearly got the better of him. But instead, the judges gave the decision to Abdullaev 36–31. I felt cheated – 'Welcome to international amateur boxing,' I thought. Abdullaev went on to lose to a future opponent of mine in the professional ranks, Christian Hammer.

After the initial bitter disappointment, I was able to reflect on that tournament as a breakthrough moment and a great achievement, particularly as I was still such an inexperienced boxer. That week I had also been plagued by injury and the physio had been working on a trapped nerve in my back.

I knew I was coming to the end of my amateur days. I would eventually have thirty-one wins from thirty-five bouts and I would say that only one of those defeats was genuine – when I lost to my fellow British boxer David Price in the north-west final of the ABA seniors competition in Manchester in 2006. I had Price on the canvas in the second round with a good shot, but he clearly outpointed me; his experience was the decisive factor.

Returning home from Morocco with a world junior bronze medal, I caused a stir in boxing circles. I went on to win European Union junior gold in Warsaw in 2007. In the same year I competed in the European Junior Championships in Serbia. My dad was adamant that he was going to be there to watch me, as was my trainer Steve. So the two of them put their trust in my dad's Ford Focus, which had no brakes, and they fuelled themselves with a series of pit stops for tins of Red Bull and sandwiches as they drove for twenty-six hours through eight countries. When they arrived in Sombor they hadn't booked anywhere to stay, but they managed to convince the manager in the hotel where the team was staying that they were part of the coaching set-up. They then enjoyed a couple of weeks' bed and breakfast at the expense of the Great Britain squad!

It proved to be a good tournament for me but ultimately not good enough because I wanted gold. I stopped all of my opponents on the way to the final, where I faced a fat Russian called Maxim Babanin. I beat him easily, and gave him two standing counts, but I never got the decision. It felt like another dreadful verdict and one of those decisions that gives amateur boxing a bad name. Steve and my dad, like everybody else connected to the team, were furious. My dad just cracked up and started kicking over the tables and television monitors, frightening the life out of the ringside officials as he was so angry. But there was nothing we could do. I knew I had won no matter what the judges thought – not for the first or the last time in my career! Ten years after that bout, I actually bumped into the English official who refereed the final, Alvin Finch, who's now the Mayor of Kendal. He reminded me that I was robbed that night.

. . .

Stepping up to the amateur seniors from the juniors at the age of nineteen, I won the biggest title of my career so far: the National ABA title in 2008 at York Hall, Bethnal Green. That finals night has to be, pound for pound, one of the most talent-filled nights in the history of amateur boxing in the UK. Not only did I lift the super-heavyweight title but also on that evening in east London you had future world-title holders George Groves and Liam Smith becoming champions, along with Luke Campbell, who would go on to be a 2012 Olympic gold medallist, and Anthony Ogogo, who won bronze at the 2012 Games in London.

On that night, Steve said I looked world-class in the way I handled Damien Campbell, who had been hyped up in the trade paper *Boxing News* as the one who was going to win it. Campbell was from the famous Repton club in east London. He was a good amateur boxer and was well schooled but Steve masterminded the game-plan and I went out and executed it to perfection, winning 19–1 on points. The shock on Campbell's face as I tortured him for three rounds was matched by the TV commentary, which was going crazy about my performance. No one had realised how good I was, until now.

Off the back of this commanding performance, I was hoping that I would have a decent shot at realising every young boxer's dream – to make it to the Olympics. That year the Games were being held in Beijing, and I couldn't wait. However, there was only one spot on the GB team in the super-heavyweight class and my rival for it was David Price, who had beaten me a few years before on points. Having won the ABA title I felt I deserved the place, and Price hadn't even entered those championships. But I was gutted to find out that he had already been picked to be part of the GB squad for Beijing. He was the 2006 Commonwealth Games gold medallist and part of me felt that he was always going to be their man.

Knowing that Great Britain were not even going to give me a box-off with Price for the place was a major setback. But I swallowed my disappointment and decided to try a different route to the Olympics. I've always been proud of my Irish roots and so I got in contact with an experienced Belfast trainer about going to live and fight there.

Within a year I was boxing for Ireland. I couldn't have been happier and I felt I had regained my momentum. I quickly had bouts against America and Poland, winning both by knockout in away internationals. The fight in

Poland was actually one of my best amateur wins. It was against a fighter who was treated like a superstar, so much so that his team made me wait in the ring for what seemed like twenty minutes as he got this big fanfare before the opening bell. Most of the Irish team on that particular trip lost, and the only two winners were me and John Joe Nevin, who would eventually go on to become a London 2012 Olympic silver medallist.

It was clear to me that I was not there to beat the Polish golden boy because at one point in the contest I was deducted a point for slapping. In amateur boxing they're very strict about hitting with the knuckle part of the glove, but believe me, the referee wouldn't have thought my jabs and right hands were slaps if he had been on the other end of them! Anyway, it was clear that I could be in danger of being disqualified if I gave the referee any excuse to throw me out, so when I returned to my corner the Irish trainer Gerry Storey told me to forget about head punches and just focus on the body. I went out and smashed the Polish fighter to the ribs, stopping him in the third round. The crowd were furious. That was a very sweet victory, made all the sweeter when I was presented with the Best Boxer of the Tournament award.

I was surely on my way to Beijing this time, or so I thought. All I needed to do now was to win the Irish senior title and I would go on to the qualifying events, but then another roadblock was placed in my way.

As soon as I entered the Irish championships, the majority of the other boxers pulled out. There had originally been around eighteen entrants but it got cut down to three when the other lads saw I was competing. In particular, a rival boxing club objected to me being able to take part in the Irish championships, insisting that I had to prove that I was Irish. I couldn't believe it. I had already worn the Irish vest but now they were saying, 'Show us your papers!'

Coming from a Travellers background, it is very hard to find documents like birth certificates and records of baptisms but I felt that it wouldn't have mattered. We even had a priest sign an affidavit to say that he knew my people from where my dad was from in Tuam, Galway, but the rival boxing club seemed to have influence. When we went across for the final meeting to decide my fate, one of the officials said: 'I don't care if Jesus Christ comes down and tells us you're Irish, you're not going to go to the Olympic qualifiers to represent Ireland.'

I personally felt that some of the Irish trainers didn't want me to box because they knew I'd beat their men. I also learned later that the Great Britain officials had been in touch with their Irish counterparts, making it clear that they didn't want me representing Ireland because they expected me to return and represent GB in the 2012

Olympic Games. No chance. There was no way I was going to go back to the Great Britain set-up after the way they had treated me. They didn't have the good grace to offer me a chance to go to the Olympics in 2008 even though I was the ABA champion. How did they really expect me to react?

My Olympic dream was over and that boat trip back across the Irish Sea was horrible. As far as I was concerned, Ireland had been robbed of an Olympic gold medal and boxing politics had denied me the chance to fight on the biggest amateur stage of the lot. David Price would go on to take bronze in Beijing for Great Britain, but I'm convinced that I could have won gold.

I took a break from boxing after that. I had grown disillusioned with the sport and I hated the fact that my Irish heritage had been treated with contempt. Having had such a love for the sport and believing that I would get a fair crack in amateur boxing, my age of innocence was smashed. For a while I didn't go near the gym because I was so upset. But as time passed I hoped that the professional side of the sport could restore my faith. I knew I had come to the end of the road with the amateurs; it was time to turn professional and shoot for my childhood dream of becoming world heavyweight champion.

. . .

It's not easy for any fighter to decide when they should turn professional, and who they should turn professional with. I knew that for me it was the correct moment, but it's so crucial to have somebody to manage you who will not only keep you busy fighting on a regular basis, but also a promoter who can open the right doors at the right time, and build your profile so that you can become a name and earn a good living. When the word was out that I wanted to turn professional, there was a lot of interest in my signature because of my amateur exploits. Heavyweights always attract a lot of interest from promoters because a good heavyweight is typically bigger box office than other weight classes. Who doesn't like to see two huge fighters go at it against each other? As a result, heavyweights can generate a lot of income for their manager, their promoter and whoever the broadcaster may be.

The famous American promoter Don King actually approached my dad about signing me up. But my dad, being such a big Mike Tyson fan, was wary of the way King and Tyson had bitterly parted company, and thought that should be a big warning sign for me. So I wasn't going to be signing for King. Another person who was in the picture for my signature was former world featherweight champion Barry McGuigan. He was keen to sign me and we came close to doing a deal but it didn't work out. Then Mick Hennessy, who at the time had a good stable of fighters, came up with a compelling signing-on fee and the promise of regular fights, and that sounded like the best offer to both my dad and me. Mick knew more than most about my true potential because he had seen me spar as a nineteen-year-old amateur against the rising Cuban prospect Mike Perez. Perez was all action and put on me right away, but every time he tried to push to another level I went with him – and that was after two weeks in Ibiza with my mates!

Mick sent the professional contract to me in the Algarve, where I was on my honeymoon with Paris in November 2008. I was supposed to be there for two weeks but I flew back home after just four days because Mick said I could make my debut on the undercard of Carl Froch's challenge for the vacant WBC super-middleweight title against Jean Pascal in Nottingham, live on ITV. It was too good an opportunity to turn down so on 6 December 2008 I made my pro debut – and thankfully Paris forgave me for cutting short our honeymoon!

I was enormously excited about starting a new chapter in my career and ultimately the professional business was where I had always wanted to be as a boxer. I believed I was going to take the sport by storm, and the sooner the better. At the time, Carl Froch was becoming a prominent name in the sport and being part of some of his shows was great for me. Before my debut, I didn't feel nervous, it was just excitement. Mick had told the media that I reminded him of former world heavyweight champion Larry Holmes, who reigned as the top man in the division between 1978 and 1985. Mick had no doubt that I was going all the way.

I wanted to make an instant impact and I did just that when I enjoyed a first-round technical knockout of Hungarian Béla Gyöngyösi with a head-body combination. After that I wanted more and more fights and, true to his word, Mick had me fighting eight times in 2009 so that I was quickly able to start making a name for myself. The bitterness of having my Olympic dream shattered had to be put behind me, and that's exactly what I did, because that was history.* It was time to start showing the public that I was not going to be denied as a professional fighter, and that I was the future of the heavyweight division.

* I did return to Belfast later as a professional to win the Irish heavyweight title, having proved my Irish roots — thanks to the help of my cousin Andy Lee, who hails from Limerick.

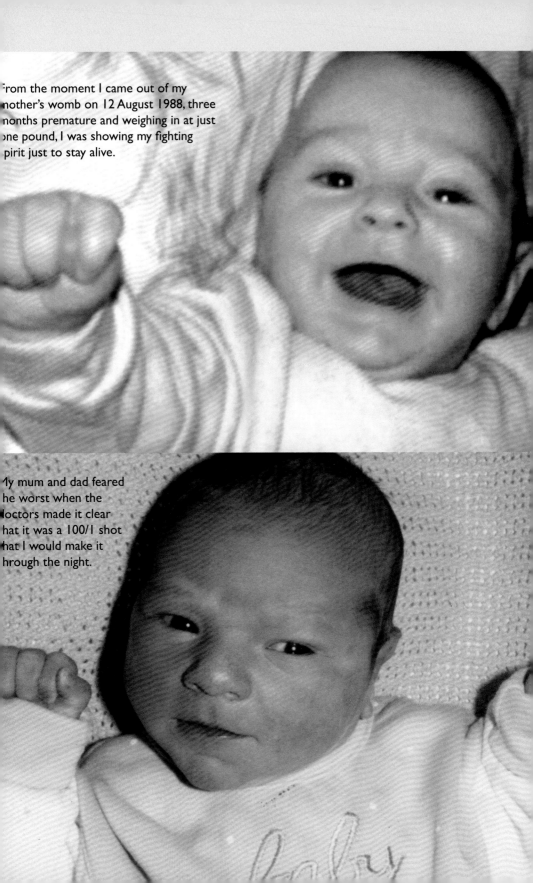

From the moment I came out of my mother's womb on 12 August 1988, three months premature and weighing in at just one pound, I was showing my fighting spirit just to stay alive.

My mum and dad feared the worst when the doctors made it clear that it was a 100/1 shot that I would make it through the night.

Baby

I don't know where it came from, it was just always there – the belief that I would become heavyweight champion of the world. But I wasn't the first person to say it, that was my dad John when I was only a few minutes old – and that was after I had died three times.

When I opened my eyes after coming back to life for the fourth time, my dad has told me that he looked at me and said, 'He's going to make it, he'll be 7 foot tall, 20 stone, he's going to be called after Mike Tyson and he'll be the heavyweight champion of the world.' He was right! And I was lucky enough to meet Mike, too.

Fighting is in my DNA, going back in Ireland over 200 years. My mother is the daughter of a bare-knuckle fighter, a former King of the Gypsies, while on my father's side of the family I am related to Bartley Gorman, who was the bare-knuckle Gypsy King from 1972 to 1992, and died in 2002. He described himself as 'the most dangerous unarmed man on the planet', and I wouldn't disagree.

My dad, John Fury, was a bare-knuckle fighter and boxer.

The Fury boxers today (from left to right): My half-brother Tommy, my uncle Peter, me, my cousin Hughie and my dad John. All fighting men.

Me on the left, with my dad and my brother Shane. The importance of a good family unit is a clear positive within the Travellers community.

I often used to think that the way we were living was something like that popular television programme *The Darling Buds of May*, where the family grew up in the countryside, living life their way.

Like the majority of Travellers I left school around ten years of age. The average boy is encouraged to get out and start doing work before secondary school age and my dad just had the same attitude — that there is a big world out there and if you want some money then you need to go out and earn it.

The Fury boys: along with my dad, there's my older brother John, me, then Shane and the youngest of the four boys, Hughie. We also had a sister, Ramona, who was born two days before Christmas 1997 but died two days later, when I was just nine.

Me and Steve Egan at my first gym – Jimmy Egan's Boxing Academy. When I arrived I was 6 foot 5 and nearly 15 stone at just fourteen, so you could say that I stood out a bit. I had never been taught how to fight, but I knew the gym was my home; this was where I was always meant to be.

Before I left that first night, Steve had told his dad to get me a medical card – that's the record book that every amateur boxer has. They knew I was a natural and didn't want to let me go. Steve took one look at me and told his dad, 'Heavyweights don't move like that. Get him a card.'

On the wall now at Jimmy Egan's gym reads a quote from me: 'I was made by God, but trained at Jimmy Egan's.'

When the word was out that I wanted to turn professional in 2008, at twenty years old, there was a lot of interest in my signature because of my amateur exploits. The famous American promoter Don King actually approached my dad about signing me up. But my dad, being such a big Mike Tyson fan, was wary of the way King and Tyson had bitterly parted company, and thought that should be a big warning sign for me. So I wasn't going to be signing for King. Then Mick Hennessy, who at the time had a good stable of fighters, came up with a compelling signing-on fee and the promise of regular fights, and that sounded like the best offer to both my dad and me.

CHAPTER FIVE

SCHOOL OF HARD KNOCKS

The rain was dripping from my nose, it was freezing cold and my uncle Hughie was passing on his boxing knowledge the way he knew best: another day's training outside his old mechanic's shed in Lancaster.

Having chosen Mick Hennessy as my manager, I had decided to be trained by my uncle at the start of my professional career. The facilities were basic. There was no fancy, modern-day gym with all the weights and machines you could ask for. Instead, the icy shed was situated a few feet from a trailer in Hughie's back yard where I was living with my wife Paris. The ring inside wasn't in the best of order either; the boards were loose and I would occasionally turn my ankle during pad work or sparring. But I put 100 per cent faith in Uncle Hughie, and in return he put 100 per cent faith in me. It worked.

I was twenty years of age with plenty of puppy fat and certainly no strength and conditioning programme or nutritionist to speak of. In fact, it was quite the opposite with Hughie. When I look back, it's funny really to think of how well I progressed. After training sessions we would often go along to the local Asda and he'd say, 'Right, Tyson, get a couple of those meat pies into ya.' But I trained hard and I fought hard, and it turned out that I could go twelve rounds on a diet of pies! With Uncle Hughie I would eventually go on to amass a winning streak of seventeen fights unbeaten, in the process winning both the British and Commonwealth heavyweight titles. I will always be thankful for the hard work and wisdom that he bestowed on me as a young professional.

However, one opponent that it seemed I was always going to be battling with was my weight. Keeping the pounds down on the scales was something I had to work really hard to manage. Fortunately, I could always fight, even when I wasn't in the best of shape. I think most of this was down to my heart and determination; even when I was so tired that I felt like I would fall over, I never let myself give in. I used to drive on. I would sometimes say to Hughie, 'This can't be right that I feel super tired after five rounds and I've seven more to do.' But he just used to say, 'This is how you feel, get through it.' It was a long way from the much more scientific approach that I would later have in camps with my other uncle Peter, who would take over as my trainer in 2012. But the one thing that Hughie was really good at teaching me was the sweet science, the art of boxing. He loved studying boxers. He had studied them all of his life and was a master scholar of the sport. Because of that, he was great at reading a fight. He could tell me within ten seconds the information I needed to go out there and win.

With Uncle Hughie we worked a lot on how I could deliver punches correctly, making sure that every punch I threw counted. Like my earlier work with Steve Egan, we continued to concentrate on my movement – the slipping and sliding that were traits that other heavyweights didn't really have, and probably haven't done since the days of Muhammad Ali and Larry Holmes back in the 1970s and 80s.

Even in my early days as a professional I felt that I was every heavyweight's worst nightmare. Part of my confidence grew from my athleticism. I've always had excellent flexibility. I'm probably some kind of genetic freak, I really shouldn't be able to do it, but even when I'm 25 stone I can spar twenty rounds, ducking and diving and moving around the ring with ease.

Perhaps one of the reasons for this lies in a discovery that I would make in the second part of my career: my lung capacity is out of the ordinary. When compared to another fit man of around 20 stone, the expert who tested me said that I was able to take in 21 litres of air in the same time that the other guy would take in 12 litres. So while

I have the heart to dig deep, I also likely have the physical capacity to dig deeper than anyone else in the heavyweight division. That gives me an incredible amount of stamina and fuels my resilience in the toughest of moments.

During this time training with Uncle Hughie, I also realised that I was good at adapting to situations; handling problems in the ring and finding a solution. This was something that would prove to be very important throughout my career. When things haven't gone to plan, I have managed to stay on track. A lot of boxers have only one way of fighting and struggle to deal with a different style that doesn't suit them. Thanks to Uncle Hughie, I found that I could work guys out very quickly and was able to make adjustments to my own style if necessary. One key factor that you will always see with elite fighters is their ability to control the 'distance' in a fight, to be clinically aware of how they can dictate the fight. I found that I could naturally find the right distance between me and my opponent, in order to be able to land my own punches, and then move out of range of the punches coming my way. Being able to slip a punch by a fraction like this meant that I could immediately be in the right place to connect with my own big shots, and that is crucial.

When I wasn't training in Uncle Hughie's gym, my manager Mick Hennessy was keeping me very busy in the ring during my first full year as a pro in 2009. I had a fight a month for the first five months, which for someone as energetic and impulsive as me was perfect. Keeping my mind busy and focused is so important for me so I loved the fact that the fights were coming thick and fast.

After enjoying my debut in December 2008, a month later I was fighting in Wigan and my opponent raised more than a few eyebrows among the boxing media. I was matched with a 6 foot 1 German, Marcel Zeller, whose record was twenty-one wins and only three defeats. This wasn't the typical journeyman opponent that would usually be served up for a hot prospect. Normally you will see a young professional box a string of guys with losing records as they learn their trade. That is accepted because, for many fighters, moving from the amateur ranks to the professional business is a big step up in quality. The amateur sport is very different to boxing as a professional, and for the majority of fighters the transition can be tricky. Getting used to the slower pace and learning how to pace yourself as the rounds move up from three as an amateur to six to eight to ten and then twelve is all part of the learning curve. But I was put in with Zeller and I had no hesitation because I had full confidence in my ability, as did Hughie.

The experienced German, who for some reason came into the ring wearing something like a kilt, came at me swinging wildly and I rapped him with my jab.

As I backed him up to the ropes and landed a five-punch combination, he tried to show me that he wasn't intimidated by this cocky kid and he beckoned me in for more of a close-quarters scrappy fight. That was fine by me and for the last two minutes of the round I bounced right uppercuts and jabs off his chin as well as some well-placed body shots. Credit to Zeller, he hung in there and he came out for the second round looking to do some damage. But I put him almost immediately on the back foot with stinging punches from every angle. Around forty seconds into the third round, I caught him a bit lower than the belt in the middle of another attack and he made the most of it by taking a knee and complaining to the referee. It was a clever way of taking a breather. But when the fight resumed after about twenty seconds I kept up the one-sided beating and, as he tried to cover up against the ropes, the referee called it off with ten seconds remaining. What was supposed to be a tough challenge was made to look easy.

The next stop for me was Norwich four weeks later on the undercard of local man Jon Thaxton's European lightweight title fight. I easily dealt with Russian journeyman Daniil Peretyatko, forcing a stoppage in between rounds one and two due to him having a badly cut left eye.

The fight-a-month treadmill rolled on to Birmingham

and another sharp performance saw me force Lee Swaby to retire at the end of the fourth round. My fifth fight created a bit more interest because I was matched with Mathew Ellis, a former ABA national champion from Oldham, which was only eight miles from Manchester. I didn't waste any time getting to work, and I delivered a strong right hand followed by a left that had him sprawled out on the canvas within thirty seconds. Another quick one-two combination finished him off. I had made a very impressive start to my professional career, and ITV, who had screened every one of the bouts, was loving it.

In May I had my sixth professional fight, against a guy from Northern Ireland, Scott Belshaw, who was being hyped up by his promoter, Frank (now known as Kellie) Maloney. He could punch a bit but we had sparred together when I was an amateur so I was feeling relaxed, and with the fight being shown live on ITV, I wanted to put on a show. I did.

A left hook to the body in the first round had a delayed reaction before Belshaw fell to the canvas and then just before the bell I put him down again with a body shot. Early in the second round, I caught him again to the solar plexus and although he didn't go down he creased up in pain so badly that I backed off and allowed the referee to step in and stop it.

Another stoppage win followed in July against Latvian

Aleksandrs Selezens and then I signed to fight John McDermott for the English heavyweight title in September. It was one fight after another in relatively quick succession and that kept me focused on boxing. Facing McDermott was a big step up from the class of boxer I had been facing, as he had gone the distance twice with former world title challenger Danny Williams in two British title fights. A lot of people saw me as the underdog and I seemed to inspire McDermott to train harder by giving him the nickname 'McMuffin' because he was always on the chubby side. He was twenty-nine and I had just turned twenty-one. He also happened to be managed by Frank Maloney, who seemed to think that this fight was going to be too much too soon for me. Not many young heavyweights would have been prepared like me to step up and face someone like that so early in their career. After all, I had only been a pro for ten months. Maybe, looking back, it was a bit of a risk.

For ten rounds I had to stand in the trenches and go to war with him. I had to dig incredibly deep at times; I was breathing hard and finding it tough, but I felt pretty fit so I knew I could cope with the situation.

Handling yourself in such a fight is as much to do with your mental state as it is the physical condition you are in. There are two things you can do in that kind of situation: you can take a good punch and fall over and look for an exit, or you can dig so deep until the well is empty and then get a shovel and keep digging in the dry dirt until there is nothing more to dig and nothing matters more than winning. That's how I felt in that McDermott fight.

A right hand caught me in the ninth round which stung me a little. But then I regrouped and slowed up McDermott with some body shots of my own. The last round was relentless and I landed some good uppercuts. The crowd at the Brentwood Centre in Essex loved it and at the end of the fight, opinion was divided. The Sky television commentators had it for McDermott but thankfully referee Terry O'Connor, who was the sole judge, raised my hand in victory.

It had been a real test and I had given the fans at a national level the first look at my heart and desire. Credit to McDermott, he was harder than I thought he would be and he was angry at the decision, as was his manager Maloney, who said the referee's decision was a disgrace. It was close but I felt I had done enough, and even as a young fighter I showed my true fighting spirit by immediately offering him a rematch.

For the first fight I had probably over-trained; by the time I stepped into the ring I had no real snap in my punches. But for the second one with McDermott I was undercooked because I took it at three weeks' notice.

Still, as counter-intuitive as it may sound, it's often better to be under-trained than over-trained. A man who has over-worked needs a month off and it's like he's stuck in first gear; a man under-prepared has power in his fists until the gas runs out.

I had a couple of fights in between the two McDermott bouts, the first of which was to be just two weeks later in Dublin. Having the opportunity to box in Ireland for the first time as a professional meant a lot to me and my arrival generated a lot of interest; I spoke to the media about how proud I was of my Irish heritage. Unfortunately, I suffered the first setback of my pro career during my points win over Tomáš Mrázek of the Czech Republic when I damaged my hand. It was a bad night all round for the Irish as Bernard Dunne lost his WBA super-bantamweight title in the main event. I had hit Mrázek high on the top of the head and it was confirmed later that I had broken my hand. I needed to get it seen to straight after the six-round fight, but not before I rang Paris, who that morning had gone into hospital to have our first child. I may have been feeling frustrated and in some pain but when Paris answered the phone and told me I was the father of a bouncing baby girl, Venezuela, I couldn't have been happier. The hand injury meant nothing when I first looked at my first-born child. She was so beautiful and it was such a special moment for Paris and me. It was very emotional as we sat around the hospital bed as a new family unit. I knew Venezuela would always be her daddy's girl!

The broken hand obviously meant I was out of action for a few months. I finally got back into the swing of things with a routine victory over Germany's Hans-Joerg Blasko in March 2010. I wasn't sure what would be next for me so I decided to take a trip to Holland to meet up with a cousin. I had told Paris that I would be away for a couple of weeks but as it happened I missed the boat from Hull and a day later Hughie called me to say that I could have the McDermott rematch if I wanted but the bad news was that it would be in three weeks' time! That was no real time to get ready for such an important fight but I didn't care, so I immediately said to Hughie, 'Go for it.' So it was set for 25 June 2010 back at the same venue in Essex where we'd had our first fight.

I'd had no sparring for the fight because I took it at such short notice and I weighed in at 19½ stone, which was heavy for me at that time. It turned out to be one of the hardest fights of my career. I won it on pure guts because after four rounds I had nothing left. I then took a headbutt to the eye in the seventh round but to be honest I was that tired I didn't even care about it. Sometimes fighters panic when they're cut, but when I tasted the blood I thought, 'Lovely. This will look good on TV.'

In the eighth round we were both feeling the pace but

just before the bell I felt a sense of relief when McDermott hit the floor after a quick flurry of my punches. But he got up and I thought, 'Oh no, my chance has gone.'

I went back to the corner and I told Hughie, 'I'm totally gassed but I'm going to knock him out.' McDermott had plenty of bottle and he came out swinging at the start of the ninth but just as he caught me with a right hand, I responded with an uppercut and McDermott hit the floor again. He got back up but then moments later I had him down once more. He got to his feet but the referee Dave Parris called it off.

I felt like I'd proved a point because people said I'd lost the first fight and McDermott had a new trainer in Jim McDonnell, who he thought could make sure he got his revenge. But, again, I showed my grit and got the job done and made sure there was no controversy. Doing the ringside interview with Sky afterwards, I got very emotional because I had a strong sense that people had written me off but I had proved them wrong.

That was a British title eliminator, which meant that a victory would leave me expecting to fight for the belt within around six months or so. But it would be another thirteen months before I would fight for the title when I had the first of two scraps with former European champion and world title challenger Dereck Chisora. In those thirteen months I had a solid win over American

Rich Power, who also came into the fight unbeaten, and the fight was shown across the States on Showtime. It was just an eight-rounder but they were showcasing prospects so it was very good for my profile. Next I went to Quebec City in Canada and had another points win, this time over journeyman Zack Page on the undercard of the world title fight between Bernard Hopkins and Jean Pascal, who was a big hero over there.

As I described in the first chapter, I had been to Detroit to train with the great Emanuel Steward and he was in my corner that night in Quebec City, which was an experience I remember fondly. That was probably the first night that I showed off my boxing skills in a disciplined way. I was staying busy again and learning with each fight.

But then, on 11 February 2011, I was hit with one of the hardest blows I had ever taken, and it wasn't from my next opponent, who was to be the unbeaten Brazilian, Marcelo Luiz Nascimento. He was the WBO Latino champion and a big puncher, but he wasn't the biggest danger to me because by the time the fight came around a week later I couldn't have cared less whether I won or lost. Just days before the fight, my dad was handed a prison sentence after being involved in a row with another man – and it hit me like a sledgehammer. He had always been there for me throughout my amateur and professional career and now I knew I wasn't going to see him for many years.

It was just too much to take and so I went out drinking with my cousin Justin until 5 a.m. I was as sick as a pig and on the day of the weigh-in I thought to myself, 'I'll have this fight, get paid and then retire.' When I went to the scales I felt wrecked. I got an early night, had some breakfast and then tried to get myself ready for Nascimento. I walked into the ring thinking about my dad and really, what was the point of fighting on if he couldn't be there to see me? But midway through the first round, I cannoned a right hand off Nascimento's chin and he crashed to the canvas. Credit to him, he got back up and fought hard but another right hand I landed at the end of the fifth round put him down so hard that he rolled on to his face and the referee called a halt, which was just as well because I was shattered and was saying to myself, 'Please don't get up!' I should have been celebrating such an exciting win but in the shadow of my dad's news it really meant nothing. From then on it was pretty tough to keep myself positive because I missed my dad terribly.

But just as I was feeling as low as I had ever felt as a professional, it was announced that five months later in July I would be fighting Dereck Chisora for the British and Commonwealth heavyweight titles at Wembley Arena. On paper this was to be by far my toughest fight so far and, once again in my career, I was a big underdog at the bookies. The general feeling among the so-called experts was that Chisora had too much experience and would be too strong for me, but I had no doubt I would win.

In the opening round I made a clear statement with the way I teed off on him with some good right hands. The second round was far more competitive. He got my attention with a right hand that made me back off but I regrouped and then we went at it, toe-to-toe, for the remainder of the round. I realised that I had moved up to another level and would have to produce my best performance to date.

Chisora continued to drive forward in the following rounds, throwing his looping shots, but by the middle rounds I felt I was in control. I was catching him as he was coming in to attack and it was taking the sting out of his punches. It was a great heavyweight scrap for the British and Commonwealth titles and we got a standing ovation from the Wembley Arena crowd before the judges awarded me a unanimous points decision.

I had taken my lumps and come through to beat a top-ten world-ranked heavyweight. As you can see, unlike many prospects, I wasn't being wrapped in cotton wool. I was in the school of hard knocks, learning my trade the tough way so I would be ready for the ultimate challenge down the line.

Things were not going to get any easier in my next

fight, when I was given the chance to top the bill at the iconic King's Hall in Belfast in September. When I arrived there for a press conference to announce my fight with Nicolai Firtha, an American who had gone the distance with some good guys like former world champion Alexander Povetkin, everyone was very welcoming. I got a great reception, better than I had ever had in England. They know their boxing in Belfast, they respect a true fighting man and were eager to see me in the flesh. They were not to be disappointed with the spectacle they witnessed.

Bang! My knee buckled; everything went black. I could hear the excited noise of the crowd; I was properly hurt for the first time in my career. Firtha had caught me with a sweeping right hook in the third round and now I was in survival mode. I went dizzy, lost my vision but somehow I got through it. It felt like a long time but the effects of the punch lasted for about twenty seconds. As the round wore on, my vision came back. It was weird because I could feel Firtha in front of me, I could hear the referee saying, 'Break' because I was holding on, but my eyes were spinning. It was like a TV station without a proper signal. I was on the brink. His corner were shouting, 'Take a point away, referee, he's holding' and I thought, 'I don't care if they take a point away, I have to hold.'

I recovered and early in the fifth I caught Firtha with a

right hand, which swung the fight my way again. I didn't let him off the hook and when the referee stepped in to stop it the crowd were singing, 'Ole, ole, ole, ole.' I had survived my first real crisis in the ring and I was certainly developing a reputation as a fighter who brings excitement whenever I put on my gloves.

This feeling was further enhanced when I met the unbeaten Canadian Neven Pajkić two months later in Manchester. Pajkić had been shooting his mouth off about what he was going to do to me but I was as confident as ever and that showed in the first round as I cruised through it. But then suddenly my Commonwealth belt was well and truly on the line when I hit the canvas for the first time in my career. I didn't see the punch coming and those are the ones that can do the most damage. Fortunately, I can honestly say that I wasn't as hurt as badly as I was in the Firtha fight. It wasn't like I got caught and my legs went; I had been hit square on so I couldn't get the balance to absorb the punch. But I was down and I was angry because I had allowed myself to hit the deck. It was like tipping petrol on a flame and I ignited in the third round. I hit Pajkić with a crunching body shot and right hook and then chopped him to the canvas with my right hand. He got up but another combination had him over again and, although he got to his feet again, I caught him right away and the fight was stopped.

I felt that no other heavyweight on the planet was in fights like these so early on in their career, and as a result I was learning at a fast pace. When you get matched with easy fights you don't experience these things, and then when you later get caught in a crisis situation at the very highest level you don't know what to do. But I have fought tough people throughout my career and it has stood me in good stead. I've got more unbeaten fighters on my record than any other heavyweight around today. I have to give Mick Hennessy credit for giving me those fights, but at the same time, if I wasn't the fighter I am I'd never have made it through them. I'd have lost.

That win over Pajkić took me into the top ten in the World Boxing Council's rankings at the start of 2012. I was going to have a good Christmas and look ahead to what I believed would be a year to bring me a lot closer to my dream of becoming world heavyweight champion.

CHAPTER SIX

ROLLING WITH THE PUNCHES

I've only had four truly tough fights in my life. The dramatic world-title fight against Deontay Wilder in 2018, the second fight with John McDermott (because I wasn't fit) back in 2010, my fight with Steve Cunningham in New York in 2013, and my battle with depression – the hardest of the lot by some distance.

At this point in my career, going into 2012, I was on a real roll. My last four fights in 2011 had been some of the most exhilarating in the heavyweight division. Nobody else was bringing that kind of excitement to the division, and certainly not the world champion, Wladimir Klitschko, who during those same twelve months had one boring and one-sided victory over David Haye. Then in March 2012 he defeated another washed-up cruiserweight in Jean-Marc Mormeck, whom Haye had beaten to become the undisputed world cruiserweight champion. I knew I was becoming a major contender on the heavyweight landscape, though as I headed back to Belfast for an Irish title fight, I couldn't have imagined that in twelve months' time I would be lighting up the Big Apple in the famous arena at Madison Square Garden.

First, I had to deal with a taxi driver called Martin Rogan, who had enjoyed his own *Rocky* story. He started his professional boxing career in his late thirties, much later than most fighters, but managed to win the Prizefighter tournament that Sky had introduced, which saw eight men line up for quarter-finals, semi-finals and then final – all on one night, with each bout over three rounds. It might have been bar-room brawl entertainment, but it shot Rogan into the spotlight and he grabbed his opportunity with both hands. He immediately went on to beat 2000 Olympic champion Audley Harrison before having the win of his career when he defeated Matt Skelton for the Commonwealth heavyweight title before losing it to Sam Sexton, all in the space of twelve months. He then had a couple of wins over journeymen and now I was matched with him for the vacant Irish title on 14 April 2012.

It could have been seen as a backward step for me, considering the four exciting victories I had just enjoyed against very good opposition, but fighting for the Irish title meant so much to me. If you go into my house, you'll see the green Irish title belt standing out very proudly. It's prized because it was the hardest one to come by. The rest of the belts I won by just beating fighters but for this one I had to spend months proving my Irish heritage.

I knew that it was going to be tough for me to prove my ancestry and secure the chance to fight for the belt, simply because of what had happened with the Irish Athletic Boxing Association, who had denied me the opportunity to represent Ireland at the 2008 Olympics, but we got there in the end. My cousin Andy Lee also played a part in me proving my right to box for the belt. Eventually, after all the politics that I had gone through, it was a very proud moment when I was told that the fight was made and that I would have my chance to win that green belt.

On my previous visit to Belfast, I had been given a warm welcome and this time it was even better, even though Rogan was popular with the locals. Those at the weigh-in seemed to enjoy my rendition of Elvis's 'In the Ghetto' and on the night I found I had good support. Afterwards I received another great reception as well.

This was also a significant moment because it was the first time that I had my uncle, Peter Fury, in my corner and it was to prove to be the start of a great working relationship. It lasted right up until 2018, when I returned after three years out of the ring. My uncle Hughie had done a superb job with me but I do feel that Peter turned me into a world-class boxer. Before, I thought I had to entertain the fans, and I wasn't that bothered about nutrition or strength and conditioning. But I knew I had to do more than what I had been doing if I was to beat the elite-level fighters. I had to get more serious about using my skills and showing more ringcraft if I was going to get to the very top. I also needed to whip myself into better shape so that I could move on up to the highest level.

Uncle Peter had spent time in jail on two occasions and it was while in there that he made some changes to his life, including developing a greater understanding of health and fitness. Both myself and his son Hughie, who would go on to fight for the WBO heavyweight title, losing a disputed points decision to Joseph Parker in 2017, before winning the British heavyweight title in 2018 by stopping Sam Sexton, would benefit a lot from that knowledge. As Peter and I prepared for that fight in Belfast I could see that I was moving up a grade in my preparation. Peter made it very clear the kind of disciplined performance he expected from me and I was determined to carry out his instructions.

Walking to the ring that night to face Rogan was a very proud moment because I knew that the Irish title would soon be in my possession and I knew how much that would mean for my mum and dad and the whole family. The noise was electric inside the Odyssey Arena as I made my way to the ring; the Belfast fight fans clearly enjoyed the entertainment and charisma I brought to the ring.

For this fight Peter had decided to make me box southpaw for the first time in my career, which meant that instead of leading with my left jab I was leading with my right. I was able to adapt very quickly to southpaw and could comfortably switch back to orthodox, leading with my left hand as I would naturally do. Peter decided to make the alteration because he felt that I was getting caught too easily with right hands in previous fights, which had seen me hurt by Nicolai Firtha when I last fought in Belfast. This vulnerability had also led to me being put on the canvas by Neven Pajkić in my last fight, five months earlier.

Against Rogan I boxed to Peter's orders and picked him off in a disciplined, smart way before knocking him out in the fifth round. I was elated, and as I walked back to the dressing room the reception I received was tremendous. It was clear to me at that time that I was being respected more in Ireland than I was in the UK – they appreciated me for who I was, a real fighting man.

Three months later, I was back fighting in England after being matched to face New Yorker Vinny Maddalone for the vacant WBO inter-continental heavyweight title – a belt that doesn't mean a lot but it nevertheless helps to push a fighter up the ladder towards a world title shot.

Maddalone had fought at a good level, mixing in decent company, but I produced a stand-out performance that night in Clevedon, Somerset. My work with Peter was starting to click and on that night I felt very sharp and composed and took Maddalone apart. Having worked well from a southpaw stance in the win over Rogan, I was back to boxing orthodox. My defence had tightened up and I was pumping out my jab with venom, dominating the New Yorker and whipping in home spiteful body shots. He was bleeding badly and I was hammering him so hard that I actually called in the referee to halt the fight in the fifth round as Maddalone rocked and reeled while trying to cover up from my onslaught. The arena was rocking with chants of 'There's only one Tyson Fury' and Channel 5, who screened the fight live, were delighted with the viewing figures.

After dishing out a one-sided beating to Maddalone, I was heading back to Belfast for a WBC heavyweight title final eliminator against unbeaten Germany-based Russian Denis Boytsov on 1 December – or so I thought. Boytsov withdrew three and a half weeks before the fight and instead I was matched with American Kevin Johnson, who in 2009 went the distance with Wladimir Klitschko's brother Vitali, who at that point was the WBC heavyweight champion. While he had lost on points over three rounds in the final of Sky's Prizefighter event, he was a strong opponent at such short notice. Unfortunately, the WBC did not feel he was good enough to keep the fight as a final eliminator so it was deemed just an eliminator. That meant there was no guarantee that I would become the number one challenger for the WBC belt.

But I had a job to do. I had to keep brushing aside every challenger before I could be given my shot at the world title. Once again, there was plenty of interest in the fight and the local papers and television were giving me prominent coverage ahead of what was supposed to be an acid test – some pundits even thought that Johnson's experience and ringcraft could cause an upset. Today, Johnson has continued to fight on long past his best, but in 2012 he was a dangerous opponent and at the pre-fight press conference we enjoyed some verbal sparring. Johnson insisted he was going to 'Navy Seal my ass' because I wasn't ready for what he was bringing to the fight. We went nose-to-nose as I reminded him he wasn't in my league.

When we finally entered the ring and let our fists do the talking, once again I boxed to Peter's orders. This time it meant that it wasn't as exciting as previous bouts. Johnson couldn't handle the fact that I was able to pick him off from distance so the fans didn't get as much drama as they had hoped for, but I'd shown that I had the self-control needed for the highest level and that was crucial. Looking back, that was one of the key performances in my career because I proved that I could box in a very disciplined manner over twelve rounds against a top heavyweight, which is what I would have to do when the time came to face Klitschko.

I rarely celebrate after a fight. I'm just happy to go back to my hotel and fly home the next day to chill out with my family and often my friend Dave Reay. On this occasion when we got back to the hotel, Johnson was there and all the pre-fight animosity was behind us, so much so that we ended up entertaining the guests in the hotel as he played the piano and I sang a few songs. Belfast had been good to me once again.

Going into 2013 it felt like a world-title opportunity was now only a matter of time, but getting that shot at Klitschko was going to be a lot harder than I ever could have imagined. I knew that he picked his opponents very carefully; he was beating up a lot of guys who were nowhere near his level. Even when the prestigious WBC title did become vacant at the end of 2013, after Wladimir's brother Vitali finally retired having held the belt since 2008, I was still kept out of the picture. I should have been given my chance to fight for that title because I had beaten Kevin Johnson in an eliminator and Bermane Stiverne had defeated Chris Arreola in another eliminator as well. I know that Arreola had a win after that but the natural showdown was between me and Stiverne. But, instead, for some bizarre reason the WBC matched Stiverne and Arreola for the vacant title, twelve months on from their first fight, and I was frozen out. That's when you realise how boxing politics behind the scenes controls so much of what happens in this business. I wouldn't have the opportunity to fight for the green WBC belt until 2018 when I stepped into the ring with Deontay Wilder in Los Angeles.

I was naturally deeply frustrated, but to keep up the momentum in my own career whilst my team worked away in the background to push me towards the mandatory position in the world rankings, I was given the chance to have a big fight at Madison Square Garden. I'm a huge Frank Sinatra fan and, to paraphrase the great man, if you can make it in New York, you can make it just about anywhere. I was going to be facing the American former world cruiserweight champion Steve Cunningham, who had moved up to heavyweight. Just four months prior to facing me he had only lost on points to former world heavyweight title challenger Tomasz Adamek. It would turn out to be my toughest fight – and my favourite ring battle.

Being at the mecca of boxing, Madison Square Garden, was a dream come true even though everything around the fight turned out to be a little chaotic. The official press announcement of the world title eliminator, which was being screened coast to coast on NBC, started well enough and was great fun. Cunningham and his team were knocked back when I wound them up in front of all the New York press guys, who just lapped it up. I felt like I fitted in just right in the Big Apple because they love an entertainer. This was the first time I had faced a world champion and I told him I was going to retire him. I announced to the press, 'This is a three-hit fight: I hit Steve, Steve hits the floor and Tyson Fury hits New York. I'd like to sponsor the bottom of his boots so I could get more Twitter followers because when he hits the floor everybody around the world will see it.'

Fights don't always live up to the hype but this one really did – and then some. The only serious problem for me was that my uncle Peter would not be able to be in my corner. Because of his criminal record Peter wasn't allowed into the States, which was why we had stayed up in Canada training until the week of the fight, when I had to travel down to New York for the usual media duties. Instead of Uncle Peter, former British heavyweight title contender Clifton Mitchell, who had been helping out in the gym as Peter's assistant, would be in my corner for one of the biggest nights of my life.

Under the bright lights of the Garden, we had some

good exchanges in the first round and the crowd were loving it. The Yanks liked it even more when I hit the deck at the start of the second round. I came out with my hands down, feeling a bit flash, and was sent crashing to the canvas by a cracking right hand from Cunningham. That was some wake-up call, and one that convinced me that I was in the ring with a world-class fighter, one who fancied his chances of a huge upset and of securing his own shot at the world heavyweight title.

Usually I am the guy in the ring with the quickest footwork and hand speed but Cunningham, not surprisingly for a former world champion cruiserweight, was the one with more speed in this fight so it was time to dig in and go to war. The arena was buzzing; they were relishing the action. It was a far cry from the Kevin Johnson fight, when I had been so disciplined. This was turning into an out-and-out epic. The referee deducted a point from me in the fifth round for use of the head but I didn't care; I had to bully this guy, slow him down and take him out. In the seventh round I did just that. An uppercut rocked him back and then a big right hook had him sliding across the ropes and on to his back.

As soon as he was counted out, I was leaping on the ring ropes and spreading my arms out wide like Russell Crowe in *Gladiator* when he screamed at the Colosseum crowd, 'Are you not entertained?' I had pulled one of my most exciting victories out of the fire; I had won my world-title eliminator and was now hopefully on course for a shot at Wladimir Klitschko. I had entertained, as you have to do when you go to New York, and before leaving the ring I gave the fans a short song as well.

Even though I didn't normally celebrate much after fights, now felt like the time to celebrate in style. I walked out into daylight, because it had been an afternoon show, with no shirt on. I was immediately handed a pint of Guinness. It was like a scene from a movie. I had the Irish flag wrapped around me and this crowd were following me down the streets while taxi drivers were shouting out, 'Hey, champ.' The fight had gone down well on TV and it seemed I had made the mark I wanted to on the New Yorkers. I also happened to bump into the former heavyweight king Lennox Lewis and we enjoyed the craic with a couple of cigars as well as chatting with former world title challenger Gerry Cooney in the famous Jack Demsey's bar.

Everyone, it seemed, wanted a piece of me. The big screen outside the Garden was showing clips of the fight all day and I was loving the Big Apple. Beating Wladimir Klitschko was the greatest night of my career but this was the most enjoyable time I ever had – it was that sense of respect for a fighting man who had put on a show.

To top off the celebrations I went to the famous

Marc Kaufman furs shop and blew my entire purse for the fight on a big chinchilla fur coat. Paris and I spent a couple of days in New York before flying home and we renewed our wedding vows in Manhattan, which was lovely. I went home with an empty wallet, a heart full of great memories and an even greater belief that my time was coming.

Another world-title eliminator was proposed and this time it would be a final eliminator, which would mean that Klitschko would have to face me, he couldn't keep ducking me. The fight was to be against Kubrat Pulev, a former European champion from Bulgaria, but suddenly an offer arrived that was simply too good to turn down. David Haye, the former world cruiserweight and heavyweight champion, said he was willing to take me on.

At this point in his career Haye had won the WBA heavyweight title from the 'Beast from the East', Nikolay Valuev, but then lost a unification fight with Wladimir Klitschko in a dull spectacle in July 2011. He had blamed a broken toe for a poor performance, when he lost clearly over twelve rounds. Haye had a brawl with Dereck Chisora at the post-fight press conference after Chisora had been beaten by Vitali Klitschko for the WBC title in 2012, and both men found themselves in trouble. But the two Londoners were matched at West Ham's ground

Upton Park in July that year and Haye got the knockout win. He may not have been a champion any more but he was a big name and brought a lot of publicity with him. This seemed like a dream fight for me – serious money because it would be pay-per-view and serious exposure because Haye is such a celebrity. The only problem was the dream eventually turned into a nightmare.

Once tickets went on sale, the fight, set for September 2013, sold out the 20,000-capacity Manchester Arena in minutes. Everybody wanted to see this fight. Haye dismissed my chances at the press conference, saying this was going to be my last shot at the big time. The interest in the media was terrific and I was relishing the fight because I knew the world would be tuning in for this one. It was just what I wanted.

The hype continued as we counted down to the fight, which was brilliant news because the pay-per-view figures were going to be fantastic on Sky Box Office. More importantly, I was flying in my pre-fight training camp. My weight was good and I was sparring better than ever. Everything was going so well until a week before fight night, when Haye pulled out with a cut he suffered on his last day of sparring. I was furious. I didn't believe deep down he wanted to fight me and I still don't, whether he had a legitimate cut or not. When he saw how brash I was and how I had no fear of him at the press conference to announce the fight, he didn't want to know. I can tell when a man doesn't want to fight.

Whatever the reason, Haye cost me a lot of money in terms of what I had spent on my preparation for the fight. I had flown in Steve Cunningham for sparring, as well as top heavyweight Eddie Chambers. The hotel bills were vast. I had been told that I was getting millions for the fight so I spent big money to make sure I was in the best shape possible because I knew I'd get it back. But I didn't.

Then the fight was rescheduled and Haye pulled out again, only not as close to the fight this time. He had apparently suffered a career-ending injury but somehow three years later he would make a comeback. That was more money. What would have been my biggest pay-day had gone, my career had been put on hold for the best part of a year and, because I had chosen to fight Haye instead of Pulev, I lost my mandatory position with the IBF. From being in a great position, with a high-profile victory just around the corner, I felt crushed by the overwhelming disappointment.

That was when I first went into serious depression. I had come so far, put so much time and effort in, and I just felt, rightly or wrongly, that my career had taken a major step backwards through no fault of my own. I didn't want to box any more.

In order to pay the usual household bills and put food

on the table, I sold my cars because I'd blown my money on those two training camps and there were no fights on the horizon, so I had to do something to get by. In the space of a few months, I had gone from being the king of New York to feeling I was sitting on the outside of the heavyweight party looking in as Wladimir Klitschko continued his dominant reign. All I could do was to try to lift myself, to keep believing that things would turn my way again, but it wasn't easy and the warning flares had gone up for the first time about just how low I could go when life wasn't moving as I had envisaged. But, sadly, that was just a taste of the power that depression could have over me.

CHAPTER SEVEN

FINDING KLITSCHKO

Boxing is a business in which you can be cruising along towards your destination and then, in an instant, find yourself stuck in a cul-de-sac. That was how I felt after both the proposed fights with David Haye had fallen through – in fact it was much, much worse than that.

I had been the mandatory challenger for the IBF heavyweight title, which Wladimir Klitschko held at the time, but because I walked away from that final eliminator against Kubrat Pulev so I could face Haye, it now felt like I was in a boxing no man's land. It was such a frustrating place to be, knowing that I deserved a shot at the heavyweight title, and yet it was out of my reach. When you have dreamed about something your whole life and feel that your time has rightfully come, but for reasons outside of your control that opportunity is denied, it's a traumatising place to be. In other sports like tennis or golf, if you have played well and earned the right to be in the final or to be in the last two going down the final nine holes at the Masters or the Open, then you are given that opportunity to show your talent and grab your chance of glory, of securing your place in history.

But boxing doesn't work that way and at that moment I just felt an overwhelming sense of dread that no matter how well I boxed, no matter how much talent I had, I was not going to be given my shot at the title. In virtually the same period that I was out of the ring, which was largely down to the two fights with David Haye being cancelled, Klitschko made three successful defences. They were against Italian Francesco Pianeta, Russian Alexander Povetkin and Australian Alex Leapai, who with all due respect were not in the same class as myself. Those opponents by that point had not beaten the level of opposition I had overcome on a consistent basis. In fact, by the time Leapai was given a shot at the title by Klitschko, he had already been beaten by a guy called Colin Wilson, who had twenty-three losses on his record, and had been stopped by Kevin Johnson, who I had taken to school over twelve rounds in Belfast.

Me and my team had to start all over again. I had been chasing Wladimir Klitschko from the moment I beat Dereck Chisora in July 2011 and little did I know then but it would take three more world-title eliminators before I would have that opportunity in 2015.

At this point in 2013, after being offered a fortune to face Haye, I was now being offered much less for fights that were going to be against lesser names in the heavyweight division who didn't create the same interest as Haye. I was totally fed up and couldn't have cared less about going to the gym. But like many low moments in my life and career, I didn't give up, and I rallied to make a comeback despite how badly I felt at the time. I felt like I needed something new, my career needed a real lift, and so I decided to agree a promotional deal with Frank Warren. I went down to London with my uncle and trainer Peter and we agreed a three-fight deal with Warren's BoxNation channel, which he had formed after he parted company with Sky.

With the deal in place I got motivated again, I got back in the gym and I was out fighting in February 2014 against American Joey Abell. I wasn't in the best shape for the fight but I did a decent job and stopped him in the fourth round. I was getting back on track and now, to show everyone that I was firing on all cylinders, I accepted Warren's offer to face Chisora for a second time. The European and British heavyweight titles were on the line and even though some people – maybe Frank Warren included – thought that Chisora would be too much for me because he was in good form and I had only boxed once in fourteen months, I had no doubt what was going to happen. If ever there was an opponent made for me it was Chisora. I couldn't have designed a better opponent for my counter-punching style and his more direct, attacking approach, and I just boxed the head off him, stopping him in the tenth round. It was an even better job than I had done on him back in 2011.

I backed that up with a victory over Christian Hammer, which was a final eliminator for a shot at the WBO title and Klitschko. I believed going into the fight at the O2 Arena in London that this was the one that would mean Klitschko could not keep running away from me any more. As the number one challenger, he would have to face me. To add a little colour to the event I had an Elvis impersonator leading me to the ring singing 'Trouble'. I made sure that Hammer knew he was in a lot of trouble right from the start. I dominated him and dropped him in the fifth round and then gave him a battering until his corner pulled him out after eight rounds. Now it was about getting that date with Klitschko.

We had agreed that Frank Warren would have a certain amount of time to get a deal done with the Klitschko team but when that time ran out it was over to Peter and Mick Hennessy. They got the deal done and the fight was on.

At that point in my career, I didn't take any interest in the business side of things. I was just interested in fighting and becoming world champion but that was a mistake. I should have paid more attention because as a fighter you need to know what is happening in and out of the ring because it's such a short career.

At the highest level of boxing, everybody needs to be working together. Boxing is a very dangerous business, your life is on the line, so you need to know what you deserve. I understand that when a young boxer starts off in the professional business they probably don't feel they have the confidence to make demands or to stand up to managers because they are still making their reputation. But you need to have someone in your corner asking the tough questions because you have to make as much money as possible when you're young in this business before time catches up with you.

This is why in 2018, when I came back into boxing after two and a half years away from the ring, I decided to do things myself, make my own decisions and be involved in the matchmaking deals. I began to realise that I was not getting the type of deals I expected, so I decided to take more of an interest myself. That way I would know the percentages, I'd decide what I'd take and what I wouldn't because I'm the one taking the big risks.

But back in 2014, I didn't know that the forthcoming fight with Wladimir Klitschko would be my last with Mick Hennessy as my manager and with my uncle, Peter Fury, as my trainer. It's sad that the split had to happen because Mick, Peter and I had a very good bond at one point, but it was a decision that had to be taken.

Nowadays, there is no relationship between me and Peter or with Mick. It's very sad, but with me, like most people I guess, once a relationship is broken it's very hard to fix it. It hit me hard when I realised I couldn't work with them again.

As for Peter, it's heart-breaking how our relationship disintegrated because at one point in my life he was like a second father to me. My dad had gone to jail in February 2011 and had been handed an eleven-year sentence but was allowed out in February 2015. During his time in prison, my brother Shane and I practically lived with Peter. Everywhere Peter went, I was there. He was writing regularly to my dad and in one letter told him that he was my father now and not to worry – and my uncle Hughie, who was training me at that point, said the same. That helped my dad a lot because I knew he was naturally very frustrated that he couldn't be with me. I would visit him every week, sometimes twice a week, because I naturally missed him. He had been there every step of the way from the moment I had competed in my first fight. He'd always believed in me, told me I'd be world champion one day, and now we were separated. Dad would later explain to me just how painful it was for him to meet me across the table in prison. While he loved to offer me advice and to hear about how I was training, or what fight could be coming up, or who I would be sparring with, at the same time there was a big downside. After I left, he would become very depressed because he was so frustrated at not being able to be a part of my journey in the way he naturally felt a father should be. It came to a point when he actually asked me just to come once a month to visit him because it was so upsetting for him. That was pretty tough for me to take as well, but I understood and he told me to keep listening to Peter and Hughie. When I look back to those times and see how my relationship with Peter now has broken down it's tough to take but sadly I've had to move on.

· · ·

In early 2015, I was regularly ballooning up in weight between fights and just before I got word about the fight with Klitschko, depression had hit me hard again and my weight had shot up to 25 stone. I was in that mood of not caring about anything to do with boxing or training. I was feeling low and hating the sport, despite there appearing to be so much going for me at the time. It was because of my depressive mindset that, to be honest, when the news I had always craved finally came through that I was going to get my shot at fighting Klitschko, that a deal had finally been done, I really couldn't have cared less. The fight was set for 24 October in Düsseldorf with Klitschko's WBO,

IBF, WBA and IBO belts on the line. But it felt like just another fight had been agreed.

I knew that training for the fight from a point of being 25 stone could only be brutal, and so it was. Within eight weeks I had dropped my weight down to 19 stone. I was training three times a day, six days a week, and living off one protein shake a day. It was mental torture. I know that a professional athlete shouldn't let themselves go that way but it was just something that I struggled with and it didn't help when I was hit by bouts of depression. That made preparing for fights even harder. Speaking frankly, I would say that 90 per cent of my preparation for the Klitschko fight was about weight loss and in so many other training camps that is also what it had been about – instead of proper boxing camps, for the most part they were fat camps.

The training preparation for the fight with Klitschko was half in Cannes, France and half in Liverpool. We were working on my tactical game-plan for the fight, switching from orthodox to southpaw, and I had brought in some good sparring partners. But I still wasn't in good form at all. I had no energy, the weight loss had drained me, and at one stage I couldn't even complete four rounds of sparring. The greatest prize in sport as far as I was concerned was going to be on the line in a few weeks' time and I was feeling like a loser.

But that's not how I was playing it to the outside world,

particularly when it came to a press conference in London, with the fight now just four weeks away. It was going to be pay-per-view on Sky Box Office as well as on the big cable company in the States, HBO, and with just a month to go the usual media hype had to be cranked up. I was ready to do just that, so I decided to arrive in style at the press conference – in a yellow Lamborghini and, dressed in a Batman costume.

Sky's boxing boss Adam Smith was there to host the press conference and he loved it, as did the media who were packed into the room. The Batman music went up, I ran around the room and then playfully leapt from the top table to chuck out Batman's number one enemy, the Joker! The Klitschko camp didn't know what to make of it, but if they thought I was just a bit of a joker, I quickly let them know that I would be all business in Germany. After changing into a smart suit, I stood up and stared down at Klitschko and told him that his reign was coming to an end. I may have been struggling in the gym, and struggling mentally myself over the last year, but I was still determined to mess with his head and let him know that I was not going to fall apart like so many of his other opponents.

'You may have fought a load of peasants before but you've never fought a Gypsy King before, so now you're getting knocked out!' I roared at Klitschko. Instead of

Adam Smith playing host, I just took over and pointed to the media one by one, calling on them to ask their questions. One journalist decided to direct a question to Klitschko, so I just immediately retorted, 'Next question!' Klitschko was the heavyweight champion of the world and I was turning it into The Tyson Fury Show. I even pointed at my wife Paris, who asked me, 'How much do you love me?' to which I naturally replied, 'The whole world.'

Klitschko, so used to being quietly respected by the majority of his opponents, was sitting bewildered as I held court. When it was time for him to speak he droned on so much about this and about that, that I got fed up and I got to my feet, offering to fight him right there and then. 'I came in as a superhero and you seem to have superhero powers in boring people to death!' I quipped as he naturally insisted his reign would continue when we clashed. 'I usually train three times a day but I've upped it to four times a day. I normally spar around 110, 120 rounds but for this fight I've sparred 200 rounds,' said Klitschko, who had reigned for nine years.

The war of words continued when we sat across the table from each other on Sky's *The Gloves are Off* and I told him exactly why he would lose – that my speed and agility would be too much for him. I knew that this would be the case if I was in great shape, but with four weeks to go I was worried about having enough in the tank to be able to deliver. But I knew I was getting to him psychologically when he denied the fact that I had beaten him in that sauna challenge during his training camp in Austria five years earlier!

The famous military strategist Sun Tzu in his book *The Art of War* says that all war is based on deception, and that was the way I played it with Klitschko all the way to fight time. I knew he wasn't going to be facing the best Tyson Fury but, crucially, he believed he was because I told everyone who would listen that I was on top of the world.

The fight had to be postponed for a month because Klitschko got injured and that helped a little, but even then I still wasn't where I ideally wanted to be. I did have a lot more energy and in every fight I go into I genuinely believe that in the ring I am unbeatable. There, I can see things before they happen, I anticipate so well and that is something I was born with – maybe it's in my genes because I later learned that my grandmother Patience was sometimes a fortune teller!

But as I have said earlier in the book, the reason I beat Wladimir Klitschko was because God empowered me to do it. There was no other way I could have won. As soon as the fight began, I had an overwhelming sense that this was my night, that I was in total control. Of course, I had to stay focused because I was aware that Klitschko was called Dr Steelhammer for a reason. He could put anyone to sleep if they switched off – in the press conference and in the ring!

As the fight wore on, I was achieving what many people had believed was impossible, but I could hardly allow myself to think for a moment that the job was done, even right up until the twelfth and final round. As I prepared to go out for the last three minutes, I knew I was close to my dream and told myself, 'Don't mess it up now.' In that last round he caught me more times with heavy shots than in the previous eleven rounds combined. I had to stand and fight to take his belt and he caught me flush with a right hand to the jaw, a punch that had buried so many opponents in the past. But I just looked back at him and laughed. If that wasn't divine intervention, I don't know what is.

Every big shot he landed I just took; it must have been soul-destroying for him. I had been hurt more in sparring so there were clearly Holy hands on me that night. I had told everyone that this was going to be a changing of the guard and that a new era would be starting and that's exactly what happened.

I had climbed my Everest and yet when I got back to the dressing room after the fight, once the initial shock and the excitement from the ring and the victory had worn off, there were not any great feelings of emotion. It didn't sink in then and I don't think it has even now.

I was there with my family and close friends and it was a special moment because it had been some journey to get there. I remember going to do a test for the drugs people and the pain in my feet was awful. I had developed nasty blisters because I had been moving so much in the fight, twisting and turning as I bamboozled Klitschko with my boxing – just as I had told him I would.

'I wanted to land more clean punches. Tyson was quick with his hands and head movement and I couldn't land the clean punches,' sighed Klitschko at the post-fight press conference. But while I was the champion I probably looked as down as he did because I could already sense the depression was coming my way like the early tremors of an earthquake signalling what was to happen next. I should have felt like the king of the world, and an hour earlier hugging Paris in the ring, I did. But now my mood was swinging in another direction, even though those around me were naturally filled with joy at seeing me fulfil my dream.

One moment that night that stands out was seeing my manager Mick Hennessy at two o'clock in the morning. Mick and I had ended up in what seemed like a remake of the Tom Cruise movie *Jerry Maguire*, when Jerry and his client Rod Tidwell, played by Cuba Gooding Jr, eventually hit the jackpot in the NFL when nobody else believed it was possible – when everyone else had stopped believing in them. I know that me winning the heavyweight titles was a special moment for Mick; it was more than just business for him – he shed tears of joy. But it was tears of laughter that I remember from that night. Because when you win a world title you don't actually get to keep the belt they give you in the ring as it still belongs to the other fighter; you have to wait for your belt – or belts in this case – to be sent to you. But we didn't realise this. We just thought we could take the belts – so we did. I went to bed pretty quickly after getting back to the hotel but I couldn't sleep and I could hear this singing in the hallway. When I looked out the door there was Mick in his underpants, clicking his heels and dancing down the hall with all the belts! Our *Jerry Maguire* story was complete.

The next morning I was still in a bit of a daze and woke up wanting to make sure that I hadn't just dreamed about beating Wladimir Klitschko. But it was real and so was the fact that just the day before the fight, Paris had told me that she was pregnant with our third child after two years of trying to have another baby. That was such a blessing and it also meant that she obviously couldn't fly home. So instead of flying home business class, as you might expect being the new heavyweight champion of the world, we drove from Germany to Rotterdam with my friend Dave and got on the overnight ferry to England. I

December 2008, my professional debut. I wanted to make an instant impact and I did just that when I enjoyed a first-round technical knockout of Hungarian Béla Gyöngyösi with a head-body combination.

After that I wanted more and more fights and, true to his word, my manager Mick Hennessy had me fighting eight times in 2009 so that I was quickly able to start making a name for myself.

I've only had four truly tough fights in my life. The dramatic world-title fight against Deontay Wilder in 2018, the second fight with John McDermott (because I wasn't fit) back in 2010, my fight with Steve Cunningham in New York in 2013, and my battle with depression – the hardest of the lot by some distance.

I won my second fight with John McDermott on pure guts because after four rounds I had nothing left. I then took a headbutt to the eye in the seventh round but to be honest I was that tired I didn't even care about it. Sometimes fighters panic when they're cut, but when I tasted the blood I thought, 'Lovely. This will look good on TV!'

April 2013. Under the bright lights of Madison Square Garden, Steve Cunningham and I had some good exchanges in the first round and the crowd were loving it.

The Yanks liked it even more when I hit the deck at the start of the second round. I came out with my hands down, feeling a bit flash, and was sent crashing to the canvas by a cracking right hand from Cunningham.

This turned into an out-and-out epic. Finally, an uppercut from me rocked him back and then a big right hook had him sliding across the ropes and on to his back. As soon as he was counted out I leaped on to the ropes and spread my arms out wide like Russell Crowe in *Gladiator*. 'Are you not entertained?'

Finding Klitschko. In summer 2010 I got a call from legendary boxing trainer Emanuel Steward – Manny as he is known. He asked me to come to Austria to be part of a Wladimir Klitschko training camp. I jumped at the chance.

I went to Austria expecting to meet Superman but Klitschko just looked like another man with a pair of gloves on; I thought there was nothing special to see at all. When we would finally meet in the ring in November 2015, with his world heavyweight titles on the line, I knew I had the beating of him.

In the second press conference in England, I stole all the limelight when I turned up in a Batman costume, and even staged a fight with the Joker!

Virtually nobody outside of my family and team gave me a chance; they just thought Klitschko was a league above me.

Klitschko was used to dominating his opponents but he hadn't faced anyone like me before. I was as big and as strong as he was and had better footwork and more fluid boxing skills. I brought all of that to him from the start.

'From the United Kingdom, the new unified champion of the world – Tyson Fury!' I jumped into the air in celebration and my dad nearly collapsed. The dream had come true.

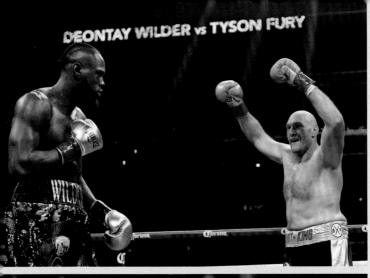

DEONTAY WILDER vs TYSON FURY

December 2018. 'You're beat, you're beat. I'm going to take you to school, you big dosser.' As we were brought together before the first bell, and throughout the first round, I was taunting the WBC heavyweight champion Deontay Wilder.

Wilder didn't know what to do with me. He had scary power in his fists, but he couldn't land his punches. I was in my groove, firing home my jab, and Wilder was soon the one looking tired, unable to sustain any attacks.

The twelfth round – a round for the ages. Wilder detonated a right hand and then landed a free left hook as I was going down.

I hit the canvas with an almighty crash. This had to be the end, thought Wilder and everybody else in the arena, and the millions watching around the world on TV . . .

Five seconds later the comeback was alive, the darkness gave way to light as I rose to my feet. It was all meant to be, whatever has happened in my life. I was supposed to go down against Wilder; I was supposed to rise dramatically.

As the final bell rang I raised my hands in triumph before jogging across to jump on to the ropes to salute the fans who, as one, hailed me as the victor, and hailed one of the greatest comebacks that the sport of boxing has ever seen.

Viva Las Vegas! Tom Schwarz, June 2019. I thought I would take a leaf out of the *Rocky IV* script by donning the same Uncle Sam gear that Apollo Creed wore when he came in to face Ivan Drago. After strolling into the ring with the Stars and Stripes hat and shorts on, I delivered a show to match my entrance.

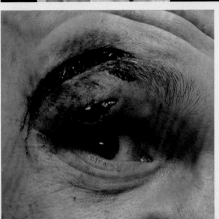

Vegas Part II. Otto Wallin, September 2019. In round three, Wallin caught me with a short left hook and it opened up by far the worst cut I've ever had in my career. Some fighters would have gone on the defensive but I took the fight to the Swede and rocked him to his boots.

My cuts man Jorge did such a good job that I gave him a bonus. But I still needed nearly fifty stitches.

had a good drink with some of the fans who had travelled to Düsseldorf. They were shocked to see the new champion on a ferry but there's no arrogance with me, I'll always be the same guy! We sang a few songs and had some good craic. I really appreciated everyone who made that trip and believed that I could upset the odds and defeat Klitschko in his backyard, when so many others thought it was mission impossible.

When I eventually got home, it was a touching and wonderful moment to see the kids again after being away for so long. It was back to being dad and that has always been my best job and the best time for me. I know how much the victory meant to my family and friends and that was special. But personally, although I had climbed to the mountain top, my fall was about to begin. It wouldn't be long before the biggest fight of my life felt like nothing at all.

CHAPTER EIGHT

THE DARK

June 2016, Manchester

'No! Stop! Think about your kids!'

The Ferrari screeched to a halt. My heart was pounding. I could hardly breathe.

The smell of burnt tyre rubber and exhaust fumes filled the car. My hands were gripped to the steering wheel. I was shaking uncontrollably, tears welling up in my eyes thinking about my kids. I couldn't believe what I had done and was in a state of shock. How had I got to this point where everything in my life counted for nothing? I had nearly thrown it all away: my life, my family, my dreams. I felt ashamed and racked with guilt.

. . .

I was the best heavyweight boxer on the planet when I tried to take my life in 2016. But when it comes to depression it doesn't matter who you are. Depression doesn't mean that you're a weak person or a bad person; it's an ailment that some of us have to face up to. Throughout

139

my life, I have found that depression has made me behave in different ways. At one point, as we shall come to later in the book, I even thought I had demons inside of me because of the way I was behaving. But I have always felt something, an anxiety that could rise up from nowhere, and I haven't always known how to handle it.

When I was a child I would often be hit with this sudden, awful sensation of feeling alone. It would make me feel worried and nervous, and this sensation in itself would then make me even more apprehensive. Growing up in the Travellers community, if you had a problem you were seen as weak. Because of this stigma, for many years I didn't know who to talk to about how I was feeling. I didn't think I could be honest, or that I could open up to anyone about what I was going through. It was really only in 2017, when I was nearly thirty, that the penny dropped and I fully accepted that it was depression.

When I started out as a professional boxer I made a decision that, on reflection now, has played a big part in exacerbating my moments of despair. I went into the paid ranks off the back of an amateur career during which I was aware of racism against Travellers. This made me an outsider, and so I felt that for me to get the attention, I needed to be an attraction in the sport, I had to play the outlaw. I had to shout my mouth off, be brash and let the natural entertainer in me take over in a shocking way. Don't get me wrong, to this day I still like to show off and give fans some entertainment before and after my fights so that they feel they've had good value for money from coming to see me fight. But in the first part of my career it was different. I felt that I had to act out a role to seek publicity, and to do that I had to be controversial and to shock people with how I talked.

To some degree, it worked. I developed a following and a certain notoriety. But playing the role of the bad guy got to the point where I didn't know what was real and what was the act. It was as if I had lost myself along the way in my own larger-than-life WWE character, and this led to my profanity on Twitter, and to me sounding arrogant and cocky when the cameras came on. I felt that I had to be controversial to make the headlines, and that this would create interest in me in the same way that it had worked for other fighters like Muhammad Ali, Chris Eubank and Prince Naseem Hamed.

What people don't always understand about professional boxing is that it is not just a sport. It's a business. Promoters want fighters who put bums on seats; television channels want characters that fans will tune in to watch. You can be an elite boxer but get paid buttons compared to someone who is more charismatic, who is more colourful or controversial, or who has a bigger fan base, even if they are not as good a fighter. In fact, talented fighters whose faces don't fit are often pushed to the sidelines. It's a dirty business and you have to realise that; you can't put your head in the sand. So I went down the road of being the bad boy. For all the talent I had, I felt that if I played the nice guy I probably wouldn't have got the chance to fight for the world title. Ultimately it came at a price, and that was my mental health issues, which had constantly bubbled away just under the surface.

Everything came crashing down on me after I shocked everyone by beating Wladimir Klitschko in Germany in November 2015. Instead of the beginning of a golden period in my career, it was the start of two years of hell. This began when I expected to return to a hero's welcome; after all, I had achieved more than Frank Bruno by winning more than one heavyweight belt with my victory, and I had equalled the feat of Lennox Lewis by being awarded *The Ring* magazine's coveted belt, which is awarded to the lineal champion – the man who is seen as following in the footsteps of the all-time greats such as Joe Louis, Muhammad Ali, George Foreman and Mike Tyson.

However, when I got back to Britain I went from being a bit of a rogue in the eyes of the boxing public to British sport's number one bad boy. I returned to so much negativity. Most of the media didn't want to give me any credit or praise for my victory because of the Tyson Fury they thought they knew. I confess I didn't react as I should have done, and I regret now how I came across at times. I was angry and I felt under-appreciated. I had worked so hard to get to this point in my career; it had been my dream since I was a boy to become the heavyweight champion of the world. But now when I had finally got to the end of the rainbow, the pot of gold seemed to be missing.

The world tells of success as such a wonderful story, the pinnacle of happiness. But my experience was that there was just a void, and it felt like everyone was trying to get something from me. This was a fate that previous heavyweight champions had suffered as well. I wanted to get back to being a dad and a husband again, but there was an emptiness, a darkness that had descended upon me.

This feeling was compounded by the two torturous events that I mentioned at the start of this book, which had happened in the year leading up to the Klitschko fight: the death of my uncle Hughie; and Paris's heart-breaking miscarriage when she was six months pregnant. I hadn't fully mourned either of those losses, and I had pushed them to the back of my mind when I was training for the Klitschko fight. But now they came rising to the surface like the lava in a volcano, spilling out and sending me deeper and deeper into a mental place from which I felt I would never recover.

I headed into 2016 in a bad way and it just got worse. It didn't help that there was no sign of a first title defence on the horizon. If I'd had a date, I think it might have focused my mind in some way to return to training, and to look ahead to the next fight. But who really knows because I was in such bad shape. I had hoped that I would be defending my belts in America, possibly back at Madison Square Garden in New York, as that been mentioned. But then it became clear that nothing was in the pipeline, and also that a voluntary defence, which every new champion normally has, was not on the cards either. There was constant talk about a rematch with Klitschko but even that was dragging on and on.

When I had beaten Klitschko I had won three of the main four world title belts (WBO, WBA and IBF), but I was stripped of the IBF heavyweight crown within a couple of weeks. When you hold more than one title it is hard to keep all the governing bodies happy because they all have their number one challengers who they want you to fight. But when it comes to boxing politics there are some fighters who can find themselves being treated more leniently than others. I felt like I clearly wasn't going to have any favours done for me even though I had just become the top heavyweight on the planet.

Part of the deal of me challenging Klitschko was that there had to be a rematch and so I naturally expected that to happen. It was obviously going to be another massive fight and I thought I would be receiving a big pay-day. In this kind of situation, often a governing body will allow you time to deal with your rematch commitment before facing your mandatory challenger, but because I wouldn't face the unknown Ukrainian Vyacheslav Glazkov the IBF took the belt away. The title was declared vacant and Glazkov went on to fight, and lose to, American Charles Martin. Neither man was an elite-level heavyweight and Martin's victory opened the door to Anthony Joshua, who at this stage was unbeaten in fifteen fights. He stepped up and knocked out Martin in April 2016.

While all this was going on, I sank to a point where I didn't care about anything at all. I didn't care about my wife, my kids, about living, or about dying. Nothing. I went anywhere and everywhere. I'd often get in my car and drive hundreds of miles. I drove from Lancaster to Land's End and John o'Groats, just for the hell of it. Sometimes I'd randomly get on a plane to Dublin and spend the day just walking around the city. I didn't want to talk to anyone. I would even take flights to America on my own. If anyone recognised me or said hello and wanted to take a picture of me, that would make me angry. I wanted to shout, 'Just leave me alone.' I wanted to go somewhere that nobody knew me, where I could be totally isolated. I've since learned from doctors that when you're suffering from mental health issues, responsibilities don't matter because responsibilities are for rational-thinking people. But if you're thinking the way I was, nothing matters. I couldn't be bothered.

Throughout the whole of 2016 it felt like I didn't spend a single weekend at home. I was completely walking away from my responsibilities. I would go out most days with my brothers to the pub. My house was getting renovated and Paris and I were living in the caravan, and she was being left behind. The drink would make me feel good at times and I would be thinking, 'Tyson is back.' But it was an illusion and the next day it would hit me hard again that I was feeling worthless.

There was still talk about a rematch with Klitschko, and it turned out that this was part of the deal of me getting the shot at him in the first place. Word finally came through that the return fight was set for 9 July at the Manchester Arena. I was in the middle of a mental breakdown and yet I was still somehow expected to defend my title against Wladimir Klitschko.

But the promotion machine began regardless. The first press conference was quite heated as Klitschko at one point told me to 'f*** off'. I was putting on a good face and to the outside world I probably looked all right as I told him that I would knock him out second time around. But the signs were there as well that I wasn't right. I was asked by one reporter about the legacy I could leave and my response said a lot about my state of mind. 'Boxing doesn't mean a lot to me because if it did I wouldn't go into training camps five stone over-weight, I wouldn't have eaten every pie in Lancashire and drunk every pint in the UK so clearly it doesn't mean anything to me,' I said. 'Wladimir says he's excited and he's enjoying boxing, well I ain't. I hate every second of it and I wish I wasn't a boxer. I hate the training, I hate the boxing, I hate sitting here speaking to all you idiots. I'd rather be at home with the kids watching the television and eating chocolate and sweets. I hate boxing.' If that wasn't an insight into my mind at that time, I don't know what would have been.

I wasn't the same person who went into the ring just five months earlier and dethroned the unified heavyweight champion of the world. Now I was sitting in front of the world's media telling them that I hoped Klitschko would have the best training camp of his life and turn back the clock to his absolute peak so he could knock me out and I could retire. Then after stating that it was 'a disgrace to call me an athletc', I stood up and took off my T-shirt and told everyone to take a look at the undisputed champion of the world as I revealed my big belly. 'Shame on you, my friend, for losing to a fat man,' I taunted Klitschko. Anyone looking at that press conference could see that I wasn't right – you didn't have to be a psychiatrist to see there was something wrong, though those who were in attendance just seemed to think that it was a bit of a joke. If only they had known what was really going on in my head and how close I was to the edge.

When we went into the training camp for the fight, my uncle Peter could see in my eyes that I didn't have the same fire any more. We were based in Holland for the camp and I felt so low and I didn't want to be there. There wasn't a single night when I didn't go to bed saying, 'I'm gonna go home in the morning. This isn't for me any more.' The sparring was crazy because I was basically just letting guys hit me, hoping they would knock me out. There was simply no way I was going to be ready to face Klitschko. As it turned out I sustained an injured ankle during training and so the fight was rescheduled for October, which gave me a stay of execution. Another press conference was arranged but this time I didn't even turn up. I eventually withdrew from the rematch, and I walked away from a big pay-day. I wasn't mentally right to fight and I felt like I'd had enough of boxing, the boxing business and everything that went with it.

Personally, I was in turmoil. I kept thinking that

people expected me to be 'that' person who they saw on TV or on social media; that I was expected to switch it on and off when it suited everyone. They wanted to see the performing monkey, the persona I had built up. But you can't be larger-than-life all the time; it sucks the energy out of you.

One man who has been with me through thick and thin and who knows me better than most is my friend Dave Reay. He had seen the signs of mental illness long before this point, and he was there to witness one of my worst moments.

Prior to the summer day in 2016 in Manchester when I got into my Ferrari ready to end it all, Dave had seen a glimpse of what was to come. It was late 2012 and he had tagged along with me to Birmingham to collect a lovely new Mercedes that I had bought. We were driving back along the motorway, going quite fast, and I suddenly turned to Dave and said, 'You know what, I just feel like ramming this car into a brick wall.' Dave didn't know what to think and kind of nervously joked in reply, 'Don't do that, I've a son to bring up.' But he could see that my thoughts were real.

Later on, we talked about what I had said and I explained to him that there were some mornings when I would get up feeling all right and other times when I felt really low. Dave knew what to say that night. He had

149

been with me throughout my career, he had seen me at my highest points, my lowest points and somewhere in between. He knew the pressure I felt and he was aware of the nature of the boxing world and all the whispers and rumours that swirled around. It's an environment where everyone has an opinion about everyone else and if you listened to all of them it would melt your head. In Dave's words, 'The "he said, she said" world where everything is blown out of proportion is not easy to deal with.' He has always read me very well and he has always been there for me as a friend. He was aware that I was making time for everybody else and none for myself.

A few years later, Dave was also the one I had to call when I arguably came closest to being locked away for my own good. We had been out together looking at properties and I left to go on home, while he headed off for his dinner. But when I tried to drive off I simply couldn't; I was unable to drive – I couldn't function. I rang him in a state of panic and told him, 'Dave, I can't feel my arms. Can you come and help me, please?' Due to the fact that I can be a wind-up merchant at times, he put the phone down thinking that I was just messing about. But I rang him back and shouted to him, 'No, Dave, I'm serious. I can't leave!' I was disorientated and panicking so much that I felt like this was it, I was going to die. I eventually managed to get another driver to stop and got into his car and told him to take me straight to Dave's house. When I got there Dave suggested we go for a walk down to the river but I was adamant: 'No. Get me to the hospital,' I said, because I had these deranged thoughts that Dave was going to murder me. He was my best friend but my mind was gone. When we got to the hospital my heart rate was 220 beats a minute. A normal heartbeat at rest is between 60 and 100. Dave rang my dad and brother Shane and they came as quickly as they could to the hospital. After doing what seemed like every possible test the doctor simply said I had gone through a panic attack and gave me some tablets to calm me down. Shane and my dad went back with me to Morecambe and stayed the night but I was still suffering badly, believing they were out to kill me and so was Paris. It was a horrible, horrible time for everybody.

I was finally diagnosed in 2016 with having bipolar disorder and obsessive compulsive disorder, which both explained my mood swings as well as my obsessive and disturbing thoughts. This came after I'd had another breakdown around the time in October when I decided to give up my world titles rather than have them taken away from me, which was what was going to happen because I had been inactive as a fighter for so long. This was the last straw. Everything I had worked for was gone. Dave and I were in Blackpool at the time when it all came to a head. He had taken me out to my favourite fish and chip shop to cheer me up. But when the order arrived I turned it away and said the food was rotten. It was a small thing, and nothing as severe as when I had nearly taken my life earlier in the summer, or threatened to crash the car with Dave inside. But I had been acting very strangely for a number of days and I wasn't making any sense. Dave could tell that I wasn't mentally well. He told me to go and get help. I took his advice and did just that: the next day I went to see a doctor and got my diagnosis.

During this time, as far as I was concerned, my boxing career was over. In a statement relayed through Mick Hennessy's company, I said: 'I won the titles in the ring and I believe that they should be lost in the ring, but I'm unable to defend at this time. I have taken the hard and emotional decision to now officially vacate my treasured world titles and wish the next-in-line contenders all the very best as I now enter another big challenge in my life which I know, like against Klitschko, I will conquer.'

Mick also made a statement, saying, 'Out of respect for the governing bodies, the sport of boxing and the heavyweight division, Tyson has made the difficult decision to vacate the belts. This will also allow him the time and space to fully recover from his present condition without any undue pressure and with the expert medical attention he requires and his close family support.'

But although I was starting to receive professional help, it was going to be a long road to recovery. By Christmas that year, I wasn't only done with boxing, I was done with living. I was relieved to eventually see the back of 2016 but even when the new year began, things were not any better. I was waking up with tears running down my face, and although now I knew it was a disease, I still couldn't understand why this was happening to me. My children were looking at me and asking Paris, 'What's wrong with Daddy?' It's heart-breaking when I think about it now. I was in a deep hole. I had ballooned up to 27 stone and thoughts of suicide were running through my brain. I needed help. I had been to a psychiatrist but even that wasn't really working. For me, I was going to discover that only God could save me from complete and utter self-destruction.*

* For anyone reading this book with mental health issues, I strongly advise you to seek professional help. I am not an expert, and these are only my own unique experiences. Seeing a psychiatrist for me did not initially work, and I found strength and solace in my faith. But everyone's depression is different, and this will not be the same for everyone.

CHAPTER NINE

INTO THE LIGHT

The demons were in my bedroom again, staring at me, whispering to me. They were torturing me and wouldn't let me sleep. They had me trapped; my mind was imprisoned. It was like I was living in a parallel universe. I was separated from the real world but there was a genuine sense that a demonic power had me locked in chains. I was hearing voices in my mind, and there was a conversation going on, arguing back and forth. I know it sounds unbelievable but that's what I felt was actually happening to me. I couldn't sleep properly for days at a time and the torture went on for months on end.

This was my state of being during the blackest days of my battle with mental health. I could be fast asleep when I would suddenly hear a whistle that would wake me up. The next moment I'd see these demons at the window. I was terrified. I was the heavyweight champion of the world and I was scared for my life.

When someone says they have mental health issues and they can't explain why, or what they are properly going through, it is really important to just listen and have a sympathetic ear. For them, the torture is real even if it doesn't sound plausible to the everyday person with a relatively normal life. This was the reality of my life; this was how I was going through agony on a daily basis and I just wanted to escape, to find a release. But it felt like there was no way out. I was cornered by something that was out of my control.

I could normally handle anything that came my way. If there was an issue to deal with, I would handle it. I'm afraid of no man, but this was different. It was an awful place to be in with what felt like no solution, except to hope that I would die in my sleep and not have to wake up and face another morning of torture. At night I would often go into my garage and down some cans of beer to try and make sure I would get to sleep as quickly as possible, so I wouldn't have to face the terror of the voices, and the faces. I just couldn't handle it.

By now I was 28 stone and heart-attack material. I would have given anything for a normal state of mind and a chance to return to the real world. The scary thing is, it could have been even worse. During this time, I spoke to a psychologist and explained to her about the voices that I had been hearing in my head. She asked me, 'Were they good or were they bad voices?' I said mixed. She went on to tell me that she had had a friend who had heard voices and had ended up setting himself on fire and killing himself. That's the power of the mind;

that's how dark and frightening life can become for those struggling with these issues. It's why I believe that more and more needs to be done by government and within society to offer help to those walking through these living nightmares.

What the mind can do is barely believable, but on the other side of such darkness is the power to be released into the light. I desperately needed that moment to come, and thankfully it did come on 31 October 2017, Halloween night.

At this point I had started doing some training on and off, but I was still the heaviest I had ever been, and I was still in a mess. I decided to go out to a fancy-dress party. It was going to be just another night, one where I would look to dull the pain of the misery I was in with alcohol and whatever else. Little did I know that dressing up in a glow-in-the-dark skeleton suit that I bought from the local dress-up shop would be the spark to take me back to boxing. It was so tight, as you can probably imagine with me being 28 stone, that when I put it on it felt like someone had just painted the design on to my body. I had the full skeleton mask on, glowing in the dark, looking like the biggest skeleton in history, with a pair of welly boots on my feet. When I got into town and went into the pub where the party was happening, I could hear everybody asking, 'Is that Tyson Fury?' I was so embarrassed that

I didn't take the mask off; I even drank through the mask. But after having only one beer I looked around the place and for the first time in a couple of years I thought to myself, 'What on earth are you doing here? Is this what your life has come to?'

I was standing there at twenty-nine years of age, like an old grandad with all these young people around me enjoying themselves. I looked ridiculous and I felt ridiculous. I knew I had to change. I looked at myself in a mirror and just wanted to go home. What had started out like many, many other nights, when I would look for any opportunity to ease the pain that I was going through, had turned into a rare evening when I finally had some clarity in my mind. Something had changed.

I put the beer down, left the pub at eight o'clock and headed over to Dave Reay's house. We had a drink and he said to me, 'This has to stop.' I told him that I would stop from that night onwards, and for the first time I meant it. I went home, and that in itself surprised Paris, because she had been resigned to thinking that this was another long night ahead, waiting for someone to drop me off in a terrible state. Around that time I had been going out and getting drunk every night, maybe not coming home for up to four days at a time. She would be ringing my dad and my brothers, frantically asking them if they knew where I was and if they could help to find me. There were times when she had had to go and drag me out of alleyways in the middle of the night because I was so smashed out of my head, or find me in a pub somewhere. I feel ashamed now thinking about what I put her through, and to realise that it was so bad that on more than one occasion Paris packed her suitcases and was ready to leave.

No wife or partner should ever have go through that kind of turmoil but I was helpless. I couldn't stop myself at that time because I was trapped in this dark vortex. To Paris it would come across as me being so selfish because I didn't care about anyone else. I was telling her that I was sick of my life, that I wanted to die and that life meant nothing to me. And then she would be looking at our healthy kids and lovely home and thinking I should wise up and get over myself. I would tell her that I was going to stop drinking and stop going missing for days, and then the next week it would happen all over again. It came to a point where Paris couldn't take it any more and on two or three occasions she told me she got to the door with the cases in her hands and the kids in the car with tears streaming down her face because she was at breaking point. But each time she pulled back from leaving me because she feared I would kill myself or choke on my own vomit – and, most importantly, because she still had that core love for me and felt she had to take care of me, even if it meant she had to go through unimaginable torment.

I can't really put into words how much it means to me that Paris stuck with me, and the pain it causes me when I look back to how low I brought her, because she didn't deserve it. It's just another awful example of the impact that depression can have, not just on the individual going through it, but for those family members around them.

During this period, my dad and my brothers didn't quite grasp how low I really was, and nobody knew that I was dabbling with cocaine to try and kill the depression. When my dad and Shane found out, they went mad and rightly so because I let the family name down in a terrible way. Then one night when I walked through the door, Paris confronted me about it and at first I just stood there like a schoolboy caught with his hand in the cookie jar, insisting I hadn't taken cocaine. Paris screamed at me, 'Don't treat me like I'm stupid!' and I just confessed and begged for forgiveness and insisted it wouldn't happen again. I had never gone near that kind of stuff my whole life but these were the depths I had fallen to. In Paris's situation, I feel like most people would have packed their bags and just kept walking through the door without looking back, so I will always be grateful for the love and support that she gave me, especially when I didn't deserve it.

Back to the night of the Halloween party. After I had spoken to Dave Reay and returned home, much to Paris's surprise, I walked upstairs into the bedroom and took off the costume. I stood there in my underpants and thought about all of my troubles and my behaviour. I knew I couldn't continue the way I was going. In that moment I remembered reading in the biography of former world heavyweight champion George Foreman how he came to a point when he got down on his knees and cried out to God to help him. So in my bedroom that's what I did. I cried my eyes out. The floor was wet with tears and sweat as I cried out for help. When I got back up I knew the comeback was on, even though there were so many negative things still around my life at that time, so many obstacles I had to face. But this was more than just about returning to boxing. This was about returning to sanity.

When I came downstairs Paris asked me what had been going on and I just said, 'Never mind, but trust me that tomorrow the mission starts to regain the world heavyweight title.' At the time, I'm sure she didn't believe me because she had heard it before. I was the man that cried wolf a thousand times but I knew this time I genuinely meant it.

The next morning I got up and felt a sense of freedom and desire for life that I hadn't felt for a long, long time. I put my tracksuit on with the intention of running a couple of miles, something I hadn't done for two years. I have always been a great runner, I've always had a great engine, but after 500 yards I couldn't go any further. The damage I had done to my body just hit me in the face like a wicked uppercut. I had gone from being a man who could run twenty miles without a problem, never mind two miles, to someone who could barely do half a mile without thinking he was going to have a heart attack. But I still didn't doubt that I was on the road to recovery. I just needed help and when I walked back to the house with the sweat rolling down my face and my chest wheezing with exhaustion, I rang the man who was going to be my new trainer, Ben Davison.

I knew Ben was the man for me after we had spent a short time together in Marbella in the summer of 2017. I had given him a challenge when we had been sitting and chatting in a hotel. I wanted to see if he truly possessed the 'minerals' to be the coach of the heavyweight champion of the world. He was twenty-four years old and a good-looking guy, so I thought I would see if he had the guts to go up to two girls and try to get their numbers. Without hesitation, off he went and secured both numbers. With that confidence, I thought he was the man for me! I wasn't quite ready then to start my journey back to the top, but when the moment arrived I knew I would have Ben in my corner.

. . .

The very first time I met Ben was in March 2016 at a boxing show in Glasgow. My friend Billy Joe Saunders was defending his WBO middleweight title and I went along to support him. Ben was coaching him at that time and we spoke briefly but it was a year later when we had our first good chat after I decided to join Billy Joe at his training camp in Marbella. It was April 2017 and it gives you an insight into my twisted, tortured state of mind that on the one hand I didn't want anything to do with boxing, but on the other I loved the sport, the art, the challenge of boxing enough to want to join a training camp.

Ben could see that somewhere deep inside me my passion for the sport was still alive. The fire may have been reduced to a flicker but it was still burning and for a brief moment it burst into flames. Ben had taped up my hands and I suddenly felt a sense of excitement. I was putting on a pair of boxing gloves again and as I looked across at Ben, who was putting on the pads to give me a workout, we both burst out laughing – we both knew I was acting like an over-excited kid with a shiny new toy. It was a brief moment of light and joy in the middle of two years of darkness, but snapping out my old combinations and moving around the ring again was so enjoyable.

This was what it felt like when I first started out as an amateur. It felt somehow pure, without any of the pressure or the other stuff that happens around professional boxing, the kind of stuff that had driven me into such a deep hole. This workout helped me believe that I could come back, and I told people at the time, even some reporters, that I wanted to fight again. But it didn't take long after I returned home for the positivity I had enjoyed with Ben to be bitten once more by the black dog of depression. I was soon back on the familiar roller-coaster of self-destruction, feeling that nothing mattered. Once again I didn't want to be near boxing and I even changed my telephone number because I wanted to be by myself. The thoughts of just wanting to die were still there. But then came that moment at Halloween, that skeleton costume, that gave me the deep desire to fight again and I sent a text to Ben saying, let's get started.

Ben rang me back and asked me, 'What do you mean, am I ready to train you?' and I explained to him that I really did want it. At the time, Ben had a few other fighters he was working with and he isn't the kind of guy to just drop someone because he thought there would be a bigger opportunity around the corner. We talked about what it would take to climb the mountain that I was looking at, and he explained that for me to make it back to the very top he had to be with me full-time.

After a lot of thought, and after Ben had discussed the

situation with his other boxers, I was delighted when he agreed to take me on. Ben even agreed to move in with me and my family in Morecambe. The only problem was that I hadn't told Paris! So when Ben arrived at ten o'clock and was surprised when she answered the door looking puzzled, I shouted across, 'Oh yeah, I forgot to say Ben is going to be staying with us for a few months!' To her credit, Paris quickly made Ben feel very welcome. Ben and I trained every day, twice a day, and a few months turned into eighteen months as we plotted my way back to the ring.

Losing an enormous amount of weight and continuing to work on my mental state were going to run in parallel as I looked to return to boxing, but there was also another issue to overcome. From February 2015 to December 2017 a cloud of suspicion hung over me relating to an accusation that a high level of nandrolone had been found in my system and that of my cousin, Hughie Fury. I had to resolve this before I could truly believe I could fight again.

I had been tested regularly by the drugs people at UKAD (UK Anti-Doping), probably more than most boxers, and when the case with them finally came to a conclusion they were able to list a series of tests that came back negative. The issue of the raised level of nandrolone came in a test in February 2016, but I wasn't made aware of possible charges against me until long after that. The body naturally produces nandrolone but mine had a high level for some reason. I can categorically state, however, that I have never taken any performance-enhancing drugs and never will. The big question that did remain after the case was resolved was why it had taken UKAD so long to sort it out. Why did they leave me in limbo, allowing people to call me a drugs cheat, allowing me to be humiliated like that?

I couldn't help feeling at the time that other forces were at work in the background. Boxing is a shady business and when I reflect on that period, I can't help but feel that if some people felt that they couldn't beat me in the ring, they had to get me out of boxing another way. But God was on my side and when God is on your side, who should you be afraid of? Nobody!

When the case did come to a conclusion, the statement by UKAD made it clear that they could not establish why I had that raised level of nandrolone. The case cost over £1 million in lawyers' fees and it was discussed in the press that if I had won the case – which I know I would have – then it could have left UKAD bankrupt. But that could easily have meant another three or four years battling in court. Anyway, the case was finally cleared up and I could seriously start thinking about fighting again.

But there was also the issue of being cleared to box

by the British Boxing Board of Control. They needed to know if I was mentally fit to box again as they had suspended my licence due to a combination of the reasons why I had to withdraw from the rematch with Klitschko and my confession to having taken cocaine.

Messing around with cocaine is something that I deeply regret and it's tragic to see how widespread a problem drug use is now throughout society, and just how many lives it has wrecked. I took cocaine when I wanted to kill the pain of my depression. But part of me wanted to die and thought the drugs would help me do that. The thing about drugs is the evil lie that is told that they make you feel better – they don't. The buzz lasts for a short time and then things feel worse, a lot worse. Boy, did it just keep sending me deeper and deeper into turmoil. That period really was the worst time of my life. I was such a mess and taking the cocaine was the shameful low point. I would rather have been hit in the face with a hammer than have taken that white powder in the first place, because being a role model to my kids and to others is very important to me. But anybody can fall and I did. I thank God that when I asked Him for help that night on Halloween, He found me a way back.

By the end of 2017, my journey back to the ring had begun, and my path to a healthier mental and physical life was stretching out ahead of me. However, although my work with Ben was going well, I was still without a boxing licence and all I could hear and read were critics saying that I'd never make it back. The doubters were out in force and I suppose because I had been off the scene for a long time, and because of the weight I had gained, they had some logical reasons to believe that I could only dream about being a top-class fighter again. But then the so-called experts didn't believe that I would beat Wladimir Klitschko either, nor did they believe I would win my case with UKAD. I had faith in God that if He wanted me to be back in the ring He would give me the strength to do it.

Very importantly for me, Paris could also see a real change in me. She knew that I was now serious about fighting again because I was a changed man at home. God had put me through some severe tests, to the point of me ending up in a padded cell. I even had a psychiatrist who wrote in a report that if my religious beliefs broke down, I would attempt suicide. He clearly didn't understand just how strongly I hold my beliefs – they're not something to be tossed away whenever I like.

I was emerging from my hole of depression and I saw a doctor and another psychiatrist who said that I was stable and that they were happy that I was fit to box. Coupled with the fact that I had started to train and was beginning the process of losing weight, this was all accepted by the British Boxing Board of Control and they gave me a licence to box again.

. . .

During this period I felt that I also had to find a new promoter to guide my path back to the summit of world boxing. I wanted a completely fresh start for what was going to be chapter two of my career. Once the top promoters knew that I was serious about returning to the ring, I was fortunate that offers came in from the UK, America and Germany. All the top people and TV stations wanted a piece of the action and it took me some time to work out what was the best deal for me, particularly as I was still easing myself back into the sport.

Promoter Eddie Hearn is one of the most powerful men in boxing today, with an ego that almost suggests he feels he's the heavyweight champion of the world. There's no doubt that he has a big stable of boxers; he has put on some huge events and done a very good job for the likes of Anthony Joshua. He made me a decent offer but when I weighed things up I felt that if I'm going anywhere then I need to be given the attention I'm due and also someone who would make me their priority and deliver the fights I wanted. I felt that Hearn and Sky had their biggest star in Joshua; there was no way I was going to play second fiddle to anyone and I think that's how it would have been. Sky had their golden boy and there could only be one; there wasn't room for two. Hearn did his best to get me to sign. He put together a plan for big fights with former world heavyweight title challenger Dillian Whyte and former world cruiserweight champion Tony Bellew, before a showdown with Joshua. But after such a long lay-off I needed time to come back and plot my way forward, and the bottom line was that Joshua was his man. I needed someone who had my interests at heart and was prepared to carefully manage my comeback.

Towards the end of 2017 there were many offers coming my way. Promoters knew how big a story my comeback would be after nearly three years out of the ring, and as the lineal heavyweight champion of the world, having never lost my titles in the ring, I was going to be a highly prized asset for any promotional set-up. HBO expressed a keen interest in signing me up to a deal but that would have meant relocating to the States. There was a lot of money on the table but it wasn't just about money; I didn't want to uproot my family, particularly as I was still working on my mental health and keeping things together. I had to do what was best for my family and for me, which was to stay in the UK.

And anyway, at the back of my mind I knew the person I would probably go with was Frank Warren, because of what he had done for me in the past when it seemed my career had hit a roadblock after the two cancelled fights with David Haye. Frank had always made me feel welcome at his shows and after speaking to him about BT Sport, who had just come into boxing and were looking to be a major player alongside their rival Sky, I was encouraged by what he said. We talked for quite a bit and overall I felt it was the deal that made the most sense. I was going to get the attention I needed, I would be the main man and I knew that Frank could get me the right fights to move me back into title contention. It was in everyone's interests that I would make a full recovery and be moved along at the right speed in my comeback. It was crucially important that I had someone who would lay out a plan and believe in me again. Frank had done that before when I did the deal with him and BoxNation when he ultimately got me moved into the mandatory position for a shot at Wladimir Klitschko in 2015.

The new deal with Frank and BT Sport didn't get signed and sealed until around February 2018. At this time I felt better mentally but I was still battling to escape the claws of depression and I was still being perceived as a controversial figure. So when Frank first approached BT Sport about having me at the forefront of their boxing coverage they were very hesitant at first. But he explained to them the journey that I was on and how I was changing as a person, dealing with my illness the best I could. And that's the point about mental health issues: you have to confront them by recognising them as an illness, a disease. Bipolar disorder is something that I will have to live with for the rest of my life, and I would have to fight hard to keep myself on the path to redemption. This was not going to be a simple flick of the switch and everything would be rosy for the rest of my career. The BT executives took Frank at his word and another piece of my comeback jigsaw was in place. With every positive step forward I could feel myself becoming stronger and stronger.

One thing that was clear to me was that my passion for training and for fighting was back, and that my life was now moving in a positive direction. The fire was back in my belly, and I felt that I had a purpose again. I was loving boxing, and most importantly I realised that for me to deal with my illness I needed to train. I used to think that it was boxing that I needed to get me through life, but I now understood that it was actually training, and the routine and structure of training every day, that was keeping me balanced. This is still true of me today, and no matter where I go now, I take my kit bag with me so that every day I at least go for a run. Whereas before I would balloon out of shape between fights and depression would swallow me up, now I know that when I train every day it keeps the demons away.

During this time working with Ben and Frank, and spending quality time with Paris and my children and family, I was enabling myself to become the person that I always wanted to be. I had never lost one ounce of confidence that I would beat any heavyweight in the world and now I was putting everything else in place to climb to the mountain top once more. It was great to feel that there was real hope in my life again. I knew the natural talent that I still possessed and when I take a moment and reflect now, it would have been such a tragedy to have allowed that ability that God had blessed me with to just turn to dust. But even more importantly, it would have been horrific to leave my children without a father.

I was feeling more and more motivated as the comeback started to take shape, day by day and week by week. When my family started to see that I wasn't crying wolf, that I really meant it when I said that I was back on track and making progress, they, too, grew in confidence and it just raised the whole sense of positivity around me. For the first time in three years, there was a release of pressure and anxiety for everyone around me, especially those who had feared the worst for me.

All the signs were starting to look good for my return to the ring. By the time I did the deal with Frank I had already lost 4 stone and Frank was keeping a check on me and how I was progressing. I had also brought on board a solicitor, Robert Davis, who has been a great help in my comeback as someone who has been able to keep all of my affairs in order. I was hungry again to prove I was the main man in the heavyweight division.

CHAPTER TEN

FAT CHANCE

My brother Shane looked me straight in the eye in the summer of 2017 and told me, 'You're finished.' All sporting logic pointed to the fact that he was right. And he wasn't the only one thinking that I had fallen so far and driven myself into such a hole that there could be no return to competing at the highest level. The boxing community is a small environment where rumours and comments spread like wildfire and I was well aware that when I signalled my intention to return to the ring there were many who did not believe it was possible. To be honest, most members of my family didn't think that I could do it because I had mentally and physically deteriorated so much. My new coach Ben Davison admitted to me later that one day in the early period of my comeback he looked across at me lying on the sofa at my home in Morecambe, looking like a beached whale, and he thought to himself, 'This is going to be some job to shift 10 stone and get him fighting again.'

The first day of training started with a six-egg omelette each – we were in this together – and Ben was stuffed! I did some light cardio work and went for a run.

The first few months were all about burning calories, but more than that it was about getting myself mentally right to handle the fight game again. Ben could see that this mission was going to be 10 per cent physical and 90 per cent mental. Later he would tell me that his main goal was just to see me happy again, the fighting was secondary; which just emphasises the kind of guy he is and the state he found me in.

Ben and I developed a very good bond. We worked well together right from the start but it wasn't easy for me. There were many ups and downs mentally and at times I wanted to pack it in. But Ben's style of training was different to what I had experienced before in training camps and that really did help me. I felt it was more fun, more enjoyable, while at the same time I was getting the work done.

My friend Ricky Hatton, the former world light-welterweight and welterweight champion, was happy to offer his gym for me to train in. And I must give credit to Ben for dealing with my mood swings in the first couple of months, even though I was working out every day. It was always going to be a mammoth task, but I was committed to the process of getting better and getting fitter.

By the time Christmas 2017 had come and gone I felt that I was making progress but even then I still wanted to quit so many times, so I knew that more needed to be done. Ben felt that as well. For a while he had been keen for us to go to Marbella. He felt that the sunshine and the whole atmosphere there would be good for my mood, and would also help me a lot in the process of losing the large amount of weight that still needed to be shifted. Ben had stayed with my family right up to Christmas Eve and then he went to see his family and returned on Boxing Day. We went out for a run the next day with the kids beside me on their new scooters even though it was lashing down and cold. It was pretty miserable, the wind was beating into my face, and Ben said, 'Look, this is why we need to go to Spain.' I wasn't too fussed at first but then I thought, 'Right, let's do it.' I got my phone and in no time was telling Ben, 'Right, we're all booked for tomorrow.' I had booked two cars for the Eurotunnel. Ben would be in one car with my brother Hughie, and I was in the other with Paris and the kids.

So off we went, but by the time we got to a petrol station on French soil, rather typically of me at the time I was having second thoughts. I turned around to Ben and told him, 'Let's just forget about it and head to Disneyland. I can't be bothered with this.' I wasn't meaning to be a pain in the backside but I could tell Ben was getting a bit frustrated. It was still part of the mental process that I was going through – one part of me knew the benefits of warm-weather training and the other part of me was being hit by the depressive thoughts of 'who cares?' But after staying in a hotel overnight we kept on going through France and as we got closer to Spain the sun hit our car and I rang ahead to Ben. To his relief I told him I couldn't wait to enjoy this weather and get some work done. I think that made the rest of his journey a lot easier!

We finally got to Marbella on New Year's Eve and I had an Indian meal with my family and some friends, including Dave Reay, who had come along as support for me, which I really appreciated. It was the last supper before seven weeks of very hard, disciplined work. Ben put me on a ketogenic diet, which meant mostly zero carbohydrates. This diet was going to help me shift the weight because it would force my body to seek fat to burn for fuel to give me energy to train. We knew that it would naturally leave me a bit short of energy at first, but it had to be done and proved to be ideal for losing the pounds. My daily diet consisted of bacon, cheese and eggs with mayo for breakfast; for lunch it was half a roast chicken with mayo; and for dinner, two burgers with cheese and bacon (no buns) and some mayo. That was it for seven weeks, with some black coffee in between. The things that were ruled out were foods such as milk, pasta, rice, bread, potatoes and some other vegetables. Sugar also had to be kept to a minimum.

I had to be very disciplined but at the same time it was

made easier because of the support I had from everyone at our base and being able to chill out in the sun helped enormously as well. The camp was beside Mount Istan and we made good use of that in between boxing and weight sessions. Ben got a real insight into what kind of character I am and what makes me tick as a fighter when it came to tackling Mount Istan. It's a mountain that is often used by boxers who fight at lighter divisions so Ben wasn't expecting me, at 25 stone, to be doing anything too strenuous but he was in for a shock. He simply wanted me to walk up the steep incline and then down again, so I nodded in agreement. But when we got there I started loosening up and then took off running. Ben started smiling and was expecting me to start walking after five minutes but I kept going and going and going. I might have been wildly out of shape but nothing was going to stop me tackling the mountain. I eventually got to the six-mile spot and Ben was looking at me like, 'Are you for real?' He told me that this was the place where everyone stops. That was more than enough. I told him, 'If this is the point where everyone stops then it's not the spot where the Gypsy King stops. Let's go!' Off I went for another 1.8 miles to the point where I could go no further. I had hit the summit.

At the start of our time together Ben had been hoping to help me feel good about myself again, to feel happy with my life, but after watching me do this he admitted to me that this was the point when he realised I could get back to the top of the boxing mountain. I hadn't finished there either, because on the way down we stopped at a Christian memorial on the side of the mountain, which had about 150 metres of steps going to it. I challenged some of the young guys with us to a race. Ben said to me later that he was standing there thinking, 'This guy is a freak of nature, a complete one-off, there's no limits.' I would agree with that!

The sunshine, the diet, the training and the fun with family and friends was paying off in a big way. Any thoughts of wanting to go home were wiped away. For the first time in many, many years I was enjoying myself. Ben and everyone else could see it. They were starting to see just how serious I was about returning to the ring and I could tell Paris was loving the fact that she could see me in good form, joking and being more like my real self. The fat was burning in the Marbella heat and I felt I was truly starting to win the battle with my inner demons. My comeback was not simply down to me and Ben because everyone in that camp played their part – they helped to drive me on, to nudge me along if there was any sign that I was going to fall off the tracks again. I will always be thankful for the support of my family and friends. That time in Spain was crucial. It was one of the best decisions

I made because it would give me the chance to fulfil my ambition of returning to the ring in 2018.

The most stressful issue that arose in the camp was having to deal with the increasing interest that all the top promoters were showing in me, as this was just before I signed with Frank Warren. But I handled it. By the end of February I had proved to myself what could be done in the right environment. The weight loss wasn't over but the Spanish mission was completed.

I didn't want to leave Marbella because it had been so good for me but it was time to go home and the kids had to get back to school. Ben continued to live with us in Morecambe and we increased the intensity of the training. Even though I had lost so much weight and had got my boxing licence back, there were still many people who just didn't believe I would ever get back in the ring. But I knew it was happening. I was getting stronger by the day. Things were not perfect but the change was coming and the Gypsy King was on the move. Frank Warren made plans with BT Sport for my return and, while the fight was confirmed in May, I had already started my serious training camp. I would be returning to the ring on 9 June 2018 at the Manchester Arena against the little-known Albanian, Sefer Seferi. There was no stopping me now. I was ready to show the world that the real heavyweight champion, the true kingpin of the division, was back.

Ben and I moved out of my house and into a hotel not too far from Ricky Hatton's gym but also within close range of home, so that it wasn't too hard for me to see my family when I needed to. That was important to me because sometimes I just needed to be with them and to have that break from the intensity of the training camp. This element of camps had always been very tough for me – the boredom and the monotony of the routine would drive most people mad. It was important to have a balance.

With the fight eight weeks away, the level of sparring had to ramp up and this was going to be a test for me, or at least that's what Ben and those around me thought. But sparring is something I have always loved and I've never had a fighter in front of me in sparring or in a fight that I couldn't work out. Few people know that even when I was 26½ stone and I heard, for example, that rising British heavyweight Daniel Dubois was in Manchester, I grabbed my mouthpiece and a pair of gloves and headed over to the gym to jump in the ring and spar with him. I did the same with another up-and-coming heavyweight, Joe Joyce, probably a future world-title challenger. Both guys are big punchers and my dad and brothers didn't want me to spar with them, because I was so out of shape and they were worried about how it would go, as well as probably not wanting me to look bad against two hot prospects. In fact, on one occasion my dad deliberately left my gloves and gumshield behind, but I still got in there. I don't like to talk about sparring sessions but even as badly out of shape as I was, the two young guns knew they had shared a ring with the Gypsy King.

The next boxer to find that out, a month after I had returned from the camp in Spain, was the big Aussie Lucas Browne. He was unbeaten at the time with some good wins under his belt and he was in town preparing for a big clash against Londoner Dillian Whyte, who had given Anthony Joshua a fright in their British and Commonwealth heavyweight title fight in 2015. When I was contacted about sparring with Browne, Ben wasn't too sure I should do it because at this point I hadn't done any serious sparring. It had all been about weight loss up to now and Browne was preparing for one of the biggest nights of his life. So I could see Ben's point, but as usual I was up for the challenge and when I got in the ring it was as if I had never been away. My timing and distance control was there, my balance was good and when the session was over I could see a look of pleasant surprise spread across Ben's face. Credit to Browne, too. He came out and said, 'That's unbelievable.'

Stepping up the preparation for Seferi even more, I did some sparring with a heavyweight called Dave Allen, who only knows one way to work, and that is to go in and try to take your head off! Doing ten and twelve rounds is not just about fitness, it's about understanding how to do the rounds, using your ring intelligence, and I never lost that. Sparring with Allen was good and I had four other guys too, including another English prospect, Tom Little, and former world title challenger Mariusz Wach, who had been the distance with Klitschko. These guys helped me sharpen up my tools for battle but I also still had to lose another stone and a half before fight time, so the work gradually became more and more intense. But at the same time there was still that element of fun and the mood was positive. I was the happiest I had ever been in a camp and that was helped even more by the response from the public to my comeback fight.

Albanian Seferi had lost only once in twenty-four fights and that was to world-rated Manuel Charr on points. But he had fought mainly at cruiserweight and was not seen as posing a great threat to me. Still, having been out of the ring for two and a half years, and having been to the pit of hell and back, it was only natural that I had to ease my way back into professional boxing again. It turned out that it didn't matter who I was facing at the Manchester Arena that night, the public wanted to be there purely for the return of the Gypsy King. They wanted to be part of an event – the night when the lineal heavyweight champion of the world announced he was coming for the big names in the heavyweight division – Anthony Joshua and Deontay Wilder.

Tickets for the show flew out of the box office; the public were behind me like they had never been before. I was explaining to people what I had been through, how I had come back from the brink, and so many people could relate to my story. Now they wanted to be part of my journey. Never before in my career had I sensed such overwhelming support from the public. In fight week I felt like the prodigal son: I had been given a second chance and I was welcomed back with open arms. To have the return at the Manchester Arena was special for me – I had always wanted to fight there and now I had the opportunity. The weigh-in was outdoors in Manchester and I had a bit of fun there when, after Seferi tipped the scales at just over 15 stone and we had done the usual head-to-head photographs, I grabbed him and held him in my arms like he was a newborn baby. The crowd loved it. I had weighed in at 19st 10lb 2oz, which was an achievement in itself considering the point I started from back in October.

Fight day came and I was very relaxed. I was determined to enjoy myself and when I got to the arena and sat in the dressing room with Ben and Shane, and Paris joined us for a while, too, I felt no nerves. I was just excited that the moment had come for me to return to the stage where I felt so much at ease, so comfortable – the boxing ring was my place and I was ready to go. The knock came for me to step forward and when I marched out into the arena the acclaim from the crowd was incredible. I'll never forget the ringwalk for as long as I live. I saluted the crowd and then enjoyed myself, even giving Seferi a kiss as the referee brought us together before the opening bell! I waved him on, did some showboating and enjoyed the show as the first round began. Then in the second round I picked up the pace of the fight a bit, but then I got distracted by some trouble in the crowd and took a look out of the ring. But instead of trying to hit me Seferi just looked at me. He was out of his depth and I was enjoying being under the lights, doing the odd Ali shuffle. In the fourth round I caught him with an uppercut, which drove home the point about just how much he was out of his class. It came as no surprise that his corner pulled him out of there at the end of the fourth round.

Job done; I was back. I had loved every moment of it, even if some criticism was levelled at Seferi. But I couldn't force him to fight – he just ran until I landed that big shot. As I went home that night I was satisfied, I was happy. Life was as good as it had been for a long, long time. The show was back on the road. The world knew that Tyson Fury would soon be back hunting the big fish.

I wish that was the end. Everything was perfect, until

I spoke to my wife Paris that night. While I was riding another high point in my career, she had privately been going through hell. She had been eight weeks pregnant around the time of the fight and we were so excited about having another child. But on the morning of the bout Paris tragically suffered another miscarriage. She didn't mention it to me before I went into the ring – she didn't want to upset me. But she told me as soon as she could after the fight. The next day we went to hospital together and the doctor confirmed the sad news. It was heart-breaking that it had happened again and we were both a mess. Just when life seemed to have turned a corner from so much struggle, now here we were faced with another challenge. But we didn't despair. Of course, we felt extremely low. But I'm so proud to say that with the support of our family and friends, and most of all each other, we rallied through this difficult time, and we didn't let the loss consume us. We stayed positive, and in the weeks afterwards we kept going and tried to live as normally as we could. And, thank God, we soon found some comfort in our grief. Five weeks later we fell pregnant again. We were still heartbroken over our loss, but we felt overjoyed at the same time, and it seemed like a blessing. The experience was a reminder that my comeback, both in the ring and in life, would never be straightforward. But with the love of my family, I knew I could overcome anything.

CHAPTER ELEVEN

WILD AMBITION

My brother Shane's big backside was in my face the whole way home from the gym. We were teenagers and it was our first day at Jimmy Egan's amateur gym in Wythenshawe, south Manchester. Someone had stolen my bike so I'd had to hitch a ride back with Shane. It wasn't the ideal finish to the day but my love for boxing and my belief in what I could achieve was bubbling over. I was gangly and raw but thanks to my trainer, Jimmy's son Steve, the sport was already so much fun and so exciting.

Now, fifteen years later, that same feeling had returned. I knew I was on the path to the top again, it was only a matter of time – just as I had felt all the way through my amateur career. I was still a work in progress, but that sense of enjoyment had come back with the new team I had around me, which was helping to strengthen me mentally.

They say a happy fighter is a dangerous fighter. That truth was demonstrated by the fact that within a couple of days of the win over Sefer Seferi I was back in the gym. And I wanted to be back in the gym. The fire was burning inside me to drive myself back into contention for a shot at either Anthony Joshua, who held the WBA,

IBF and WBO titles, or the WBC heavyweight champion Deontay Wilder.

Fighters have come back before after long lay-offs, but no one had recovered from being in the kind of mental state that I had been in and returned to the summit of the sport. I believed that I was ready to do just that. Before, I would have had a blow-out after a fight, eating and drinking heavily for weeks. I would have put on so much weight and then I would have had to go through the torture again of losing 5 stone, but not now. I was spending quality time with my family, loving seeing the kids having fun with me and each other. I enjoyed being fit again, as well as all the banter in the gym. I was therefore delighted when Frank Warren announced that I would be facing Italian Francesco Pianeta at Windsor Park in Belfast, where the Northern Ireland football team play. Carl Frampton is a two-weight world champion and Northern Ireland hero and he had a big fight against the Australian Luke Jackson in the main event, which would see the winner going on to face Leeds star Josh Warrington, the IBF featherweight champion. I was part of a huge bill, which also boasted the two-time Irish Olympic bronze medallist Paddy Barnes, who was fighting for the WBC flyweight title. The press conference to announce the fight was buzzing and the media interest was huge. I was very excited about having a step up in class from Seferi.

Pianeta and I had sparred in 2012 when he was unbeaten, and I had been impressed with him. He went on to fight Wladimir Klitschko for the world title in 2013, losing in six rounds. He would go on to lose against another decent heavyweight, Ruslan Chagaev, but by the summer of 2018 he had seen better days. Still, for me he looked an ideal opponent considering I was still making my comeback.

When a fighter is returning to the ring after a long lay-off, he has to take time to build himself back up to title contention. Sometimes the public might not quite understand why certain fights are made, but a fighter must be given time to feel what it is like to box round after round, to handle being back under the lights.

The Seferi bout got me going again but to be ready for Pianeta my trainer Ben stepped up the intensity of the sparring. It wasn't easy getting sparring sessions to prepare me for a 6 foot 5 southpaw opponent, but I had five different sparring partners and that got me in decent shape for the fight, which came just two months after my comeback win in the Manchester Arena. I felt I was making the steady progress that was required, but then about four weeks before the fight in Belfast I got a phone call from Frank Warren to say that he could make a deal for me to fight Deontay Wilder for the WBC heavyweight championship before Christmas. It was a bolt from the blue and obviously well ahead of the schedule I had in my mind. But I didn't hesitate – I told Frank to make the fight.

At this point there had been a lot of talk back and forth between Anthony Joshua and his promoter and Wilder's team. Wilder is looked after by promoter Shelly Finkel and I understand that he had put together an offer for Joshua – with some help from Frank Warren – to face Wilder for what would have been the undisputed heavyweight championship of the world. It was a fight that the world wanted to see and I believe Joshua would have been offered a guaranteed purse of tens of millions of dollars, plus a very attractive rematch clause if he lost. It seemed like too good an offer to turn down, but I understand that that's what Joshua's team did. Despite all that money, I believe Joshua backed away. People can draw their own conclusions. But Eddie Hearn continued to say that the reason the fight didn't happen was down to the Wilder camp. Joshua, instead, signed to fight Alexander Povetkin at Wembley and that opened a window of opportunity for me.

It didn't take long for Frank and Shelly to get a deal done, simply because both Wilder and I wanted to fight. I may have been still working through my mental health issues, and I may have still been waiting for my second comeback fight against an average opponent. But in the same way that I had offered to fight Joshua in my first fight back, and had said I would never duck any challenge, my fighting heart now was not going to allow me to turn down the mammoth challenge of taking on Wilder, who had a perfect record of thirty-nine wins and thirty-nine knockouts.

By the time I arrived in Belfast for the Pianeta fight, all the talk was about me going on to fight Wilder if I could get past Pianeta. At the pre-fight press conference there was a real buzz. Behind the scenes the Wilder negotiations were coming to a close and word came through that Wilder would be at ringside doing commentary for BT Sport, who were screening the bill. His promoter Shelly Finkel would also be at ringside.

I was in good form at the press conference, promising the Belfast public that they would be witnessing 'a heavyweight Sugar Ray Leonard' against Pianeta, who would be turned into 'spicy meatballs'. The Belfast public had always given me a great reception on the three occasions that I had boxed there before and it was even better this time. I walked out of the hotel for a walk with my team and as I was crossing the road the cars were tooting and calling out, 'Go on, the Gypsy King!' It's a great boxing city, Belfast, and I could feel how much the people wanted me to do well in my comeback. I was signing hundreds of autographs and having loads of selfies taken everywhere I went.

Knowing that the Wilder fight was virtually agreed, I knew I had to raise my game for this second fight. There was no time to waste and I had to get the maximum out of the performance to give myself a chance of beating the WBC champion.

Wilder, who calls himself 'The Bronze Bomber', got into Belfast in time for my weigh-in and he cranked up the hype with his screams of 'Bomb Squad!', which was darkly ironic because we were in the Europa Hotel, which is one of the most bombed hotels in Europe, having suffered badly throughout the Troubles. My dad was on the stage and could see Wilder taunting me with his shouts of 'Bomb Squad' so he started answering him back and had a right go at Wilder himself before being pulled back by my trainer, Ben. It was the start of what was going to be weeks of hype and it continued in the lobby of the hotel. Both Wilder and I were caught in the middle of hundreds of fans and security guys as we traded insults and promised to knock each other out. We hadn't even signed on the dotted line but the pre-fight hype had started.

I still had a job to do and that was to defeat Pianeta. As I stepped out on to the Windsor Park pitch the reception was incredible. I had a great welcome back in Manchester and I have to say the ringwalk in Belfast was epic, second to none. The fans were amazing. There were about 25,000 in the arena and they were letting the Gypsy King feel the love.

The key point about this fight for me was about getting more rounds under my belt. If the Wilder fight was going to happen next, I had to know what it was like to go ten rounds at a good pace and that's what I did against Pianeta. Throughout the fight I listened to Ben and stayed focused on the things I wanted to work on. I didn't look out of the ring and mess about at all, the way I had done against Seferi – I just worked hard throughout the fight. My movement was good, I was slipping shots very well and could feel that things were starting to click again.

The fans probably wanted to see a stoppage but I was delighted with my performance. The fireworks then kicked off again with Wilder when he stepped through the ropes and we told the world that the fight was going to happen. The verbal assaults were heard across the arena and the fans loved it, shouting, 'Go on, Tyson!' The rain was coming down but the Irish supporters loved the whole event. Paddy Barnes unfortunately lost his big fight but Carl Frampton got his victory to cap a special evening.

When and where the Wilder fight would happen still had to be decided, and all the issues that go into making a big fight still had to be signed and sealed. That led to some people, most notably Eddie Hearn, stating that the fight would not take place. He, like many others, just couldn't get his head around the fact that I had the confidence and would be able to whip myself into the shape needed to take on Wilder. Maybe he also just couldn't accept that I had exposed all the talk from the Joshua camp that it was too hard to get a deal done with Wilder.

The moment of truth arrived when I was sitting at home with Ben and the word came through that the deal had been agreed. I told Ben, who wasn't entirely happy because he naturally believed that I needed more time to be ready for Wilder. He knew that at 100 per cent I would beat Wilder every day of the week and just felt that although I was making good progress it was coming too soon – that after the fight with Pianeta I would need more time to rest. Initially, the Wilder fight was made for November 2018 but we got it pushed back to 1 December. If Ben was a bit annoyed at how quickly the fight had come around, that was nothing to what I walked into when I told my dad, John.

Having been a professional heavyweight himself, my dad knows boxing. He knows all about the dirty side of the politics that go on behind the scenes and also what it takes to be ready for a big fight. So when I told him I was fighting Wilder he went ballistic. My dad's a straight-talker and as my father and a man who knows the sport, he didn't hold back about what Wilder could do to me. He told me that I would get knocked out and that I could get brain damage, and then what would happen to my children, who wouldn't have a father to look after them? He didn't let up, telling me, 'Look at Wilder and look at the two guys you've beaten; he's at a different level. The guy could kill you.' He then told me that if I was going to go through with the Wilder fight, he wouldn't speak to me.

True to his word, for the last seven weeks of camp leading up to the bout on 1 December in the Staples Center, Los Angeles, my dad didn't talk to me. That was difficult for me; it obviously upset me. It wasn't a good time because everything else had gone so well up until that point in my comeback, but I had to just focus on the challenge and what I needed to do in order to become heavyweight champion of the world again.

My dad's fears were the concerns of a father for a son. He told me that he was warning me out of love because he couldn't care less about the fame and the fortune, and I accepted that. I suppose that looking back, I can understand why people within the sport did not believe it would take place, thinking only a fool would have taken that fight against such a dangerous man like Wilder, having been out of the ring so long and with only two easy fights in the tank. But my innate defiance that had led me to overcome Wladimir Klitschko against all the odds made me believe that I could go to the States and conquer Wilder.

Such a big fight always requires the fighters to go on a media tour. It was going to be on pay-per-view in America and back home in the UK. To make sure it became the huge event it deserved to be, Wilder and myself had to play our part in generating interest. This was going to be the biggest fight of 2018 – Wilder, the undefeated WBC heavyweight champion of the world, against me, the undefeated lineal world heavyweight champion.

The first official press conference was held in London at the BT TV offices, and we got right down to it, letting each other know what the other could expect when we got into the ring. One thing I knew, and I made it clear to Wilder, was that the only reason he was facing me was because his team felt – just like my dad and many of those around me – that by all boxing logic I couldn't be in the right sort of shape to beat him. From Wilder's point of view, it was the right time to get me, rather than wait for another year when I would be in top shape. Beating the Gypsy King would elevate his profile in America and around the world.

Wilder was a good dance partner at the media events. We had two more stops on our tour, in New York and then finally in Los Angeles. He's brash and loud and was the first guy who could really have a good verbal go back at me. Wilder's very confident in his ability and he should be, because he's one of the hardest-punching heavyweights of all time – maybe the hardest.

I enjoyed the whole build-up, giving the Americans a taste of what was to come in fight week. But when that was wrapped up, my team and I had to get down to the hard work of preparing for the challenge ahead. One of the big decisions that had to be made was where to train Stateside. Ben and I both agreed that we should head to the Big Bear Mountain training camp, which has been used by many elite fighters over the years. About two months before the fight we were hidden away in a cabin up the mountain, just like when I was preparing to fight Wladimir Klitschko and I had spent a large part of my training camp in a forest in Holland. However, this time at Big Bear there were two big differences – one being the fact that it took a week for my body clock to get used to the new time zone. I was waking up at 4.30 a.m. and wondering where I could go for something to eat! The other difference was the fact that we were at altitude and that had a major impact on my body.

Neither Ben nor I quite knew what to expect from training at altitude but it was really tough. It felt like there was no air and I couldn't spar six rounds because I couldn't breathe properly. That created some negativity and a lot of concern from my team, and I could sense it from Ben when we were working on the pads. We had organised some very good sparring partners, including top prospect Joe Joyce. But because of the altitude I was sparring one-paced, which isn't me because anyone who has seen me fight knows that my speed, my movement and my reflexes are my key attributes, and honing these was going to be vital for my fight with Wilder. So the signs were far from good – and it couldn't be forgotten that my body had naturally been drained by the loss of 10 stone in the space of twelve months.

The training camp at Big Bear had seemed like a great idea. But now it was starting to look as though the gamble of my life to become world heavyweight champion of the world – just five months after my first fight in two and a half years – was going to crash and burn. That was the negative vibe that had built up and up among my team over the weeks. Some of the guys were suggesting that we go back to town, back to sea level, to continue the camp, to see if I could get the spark back into my boxing. We also wanted to figure out if the altitude work had actually improved my fitness. I couldn't tell if my fitness was on track due to feeling so tired in the gym.

Ben insisted we needed a change. At first, I didn't want to leave. I didn't want anyone to think that, somehow, I had backed away from a challenge, but that wasn't the case. Ben just knew that the mood in the camp had to be lifted. During the Los Angeles stage of our media tour we had arranged to train at the Wild Card gym, which is run by the legendary trainer Freddie Roach, who has a string of

During the depths of my depression I was 28 stone and heart-attack material. I would have given anything for a normal state of mind and a chance to return to the real world.

I first met Paris, the love of my life, in 2005 at a wedding in London. Paris was fifteen and I was seventeen. Right away I felt drawn to her but the feeling didn't seem to be mutual at first!

Thankfully we met again and we clicked. We got married very young — I was twenty and Paris was eighteen.

When I reflect on the life I have had with Paris, I am aware just how blessed I am to have her by my side and how blessed our children are to have her as a mother.

A close family unit is worth more than gold. Since my depression, I have come to appreciate more and more the simple things in life, to appreciate my family more than ever – whether that's enjoying a lunch together or a holiday with the kids.

My comeback was not simply down to me and Ben. In particular, everyone in my Marbella training camps played their part – they helped to drive me on, to nudge me along if there was any sign that I was going to fall off the tracks again. I will always be thankful for the support of my family and friends.

My trainer Ben Davison has also suffered from depression, and that's one of the reasons why he has been so good for me during my comeback: he can read the signs in me when I'm not in a great place, and he knows exactly how to respond. Crucially, Ben has understood me.

Team Tyson: my friends, fellow boxers, trainers and my promoters – Frank Warren and Bob Arum (bottom picture).

I've worked incredibly hard to come back, but I've enjoyed it, too. I've made lots of new friends along the way!

When the WWE opportunity came up I just thought, 'Why not?' For my son Prince it was a dream come true. He plays WWE on his PlayStation every single day and when he got to meet the superstars backstage, including The Rock, it was amazing for him. I was the best dad ever!

I had the challenge of facing the so-called 'Monster Among Men' Braun Strowman in the wrestling ring. We made a family holiday out of it in October 2019, and Paris and I and the five children flew out to Orlando, Florida, to the WWE's Performance Center. There the wrestlers train and learn how to look after themselves in the ring, and I can confirm that it's a lot more intense than people would think – and pretty sore on the back!

world champions to his name – including the great Manny Pacquiao. We had dinner that night with Freddie, and Ben suggested we should bring him in for the lead-up to the fight and for the night itself, and I agreed. It seemed like a good idea to have someone with his experience around the camp. With that agreed we automatically thought of Freddie's Wild Card gym to finish off the last four weeks of camp when it was time to leave Big Bear.

Everyone was concerned because my preparation had gone badly up until this point. I wasn't sparring well but I told my team not to worry and that I would rise to the occasion, as I always do. Sparring isn't fighting and I said, 'Just let me get through the camp injury-free and I'll do the rest.' I'll admit that I wasn't feeling particularly sharp or strong but I knew that winning and losing is in the mind – and my mentality was 'win, win, win'. I can't control what judges and referees do but my mindset is always to win – you'll never beat me in that department. In my situation, because of the bad training camp, some fighters may have pulled out and looked to postpone the fight for a couple of months, but there was no way I was doing that.

Thankfully, once I started working in Freddie's gym, the whole vibe around the camp transformed. I was back up on my toes in sparring, the spring was back in my step and although I had feared about my overall condition while training in Big Bear, it had turned out for the best. My fitness was spot on and the tough training had given me the energy and conditioning that I was going to need for twelve hard rounds with Wilder. We rented a house in Hollywood Hills. It was a better environment and we had sunshine every day. Sparring got easier and the negativity lifted.

The whole experience in LA was very positive. I was running every morning where the stars run in Hollywood, with the sun on my back. I was getting flown around the place in a helicopter, which was laid on by Wilder's team, who were staging the event. They were very fair people and it felt good. I was being treated like a champion for the first time in my career and it just added to the good mood that was rising within the camp. On the weekends I would go to Beverly Hills, heading down Rodeo Drive and Canon Drive and sharing enjoyable meals with the team.

Although my first impressions of Hollywood were golden, there was a reality check to the place as well. Just a few miles away from where we and some of the big-screen stars would be having a tasty lunch was Hollywood Boulevard, home to thousands of homeless people. I thought it was like a third world country. They call it Skid Row because of the blocks and blocks of people who are homeless, many of whom suffer with mental health problems and are often without support or hope. It felt so unjust that up the road there was all this wealth. The homeless there are mainly black and Hispanic people. They have no toilets, no money, no help; nobody cares about them. They call it the place of broken stars because so many young people go there to try and make it as an actor but, after ten years of trying, they end up with nothing and they have nowhere else to go. Their dreams are finished and it's such a shame.

I never understood the song 'Hotel California' by the Eagles before I witnessed that poverty and hopelessness. The hotel in the song is Los Angeles and those homeless people have ended up broken . . . they have checked in but they can never leave because there is nowhere else to go but Skid Row.

By the grace of God, I had risen from my own Skid Row to the point where I was only days away from once more having the heavyweight title within my grasp. I had come to Hollywood to chase my own dream, to prove to the world that I was an A-list champion of the ring once more. I was back in the big time with the chance to write my own script and there was no way that I was going to fluff my lines against Wilder.

CHAPTER TWELVE

DRAWING POWER

Boxing: it's a sport, but not as you know it; or certainly not as you might imagine a sport to be. It's not like a football match or tournament, in which you can come back the next week or the next season and have another go. In the fight business, it is so often now or never. I'm not in any way criticising other sports; at the top level they all have their challenges. But my moment had come.

When fight week arrives, the full enormity of what you're doing smacks you between the eyes and digs you in the gut. You're fighting for your life, it's all on the line. It doesn't matter who you're facing; with a few days to go I almost always get the same sickening feeling. I got it before facing Deontay Wilder and before so many other fights too. It's almost a sense of helplessness as you face your destiny. I think boxing might be a little like childbirth – after it you think, 'I don't want to do that again.' But you know it was worth it, and that it means so much (although some mothers out there may argue that us boxers have it easy!).

As a fighter, you're aware that you may not come out of the ring the same person, or even alive. You could do so much damage to an opponent that they may never see their family again and yet you have signed up for this – this is your profession and you must walk out to the ring under the bright lights and with the world watching. This is the dread, the cold reality of being a fighting man. But then afterwards, after you have had your hand raised, after the belt has been lifted above your head and you have come through safely, you are ready to go through the torture again.

The build-up to a big fight – the media commitments, the hype, the sense of anticipation of glory or defeat, and the actual fight itself over twelve rounds – can leave a boxer emotionally and physically exhausted. That's why the majority of boxers will immediately go on holiday after a fight. After such an intense period, from the start of camp to the final bell, they need that release. The intensity of a camp and the camaraderie of a team over a period of roughly twelve weeks is followed by the lonely battle in the ring. That roped-off square is a relentlessly unforgiving place – there's nowhere to hide, there's nobody that you as a fighter can pass the proverbial 'ball' to, there's nobody to give you a breather. It's down to you, and while it's not something that you can allow yourself to contemplate, you know that at any moment you could be rendered unconscious and never fully recover. This is the risk for every boxer. All a fighter has is transported into that ring, and that's why many fighters can become paranoid about people around them, wondering who really cares about them as they put their body in harm's way. This is a business and you can't take it personally. That's something that took me a long time to accept. You do what you have to do in order to make this business work for yourself, and you realise that there are very, very few people that you can call true friends.

When it comes to fight night there is nobody more confident about going through those ropes to meet any challenger than me, but I'm flesh and blood like everyone else and a few days out from the Wilder fight I had the thoughts that I have had so often before. The fight was looming large. There was a sense of no way back; it was now about winning or losing. Wilder may well have been the hardest puncher on the planet, but for me it wasn't about getting knocked down or even knocked out, because that can happen in sparring and it doesn't matter – that's part of boxing. This was about my future, about my unbeaten record, about my pride as a fighting man, and finally, about leaving the ring with my brain intact. Admitting this sounds like weakness, but it's the cold, hard truth of the life of every boxer.

When it comes to handling the media during fight week, as well as your own expectations and fears, your self-belief and psychological toughness has to kick in. You have to remind yourself who you are and about the ability that you possess. In this department I do not believe I can be toppled by anyone, and this was something that hit home to my trainer Ben Davison more than ever during the final few days leading up to my clash with Wilder on 1 December 2018 at the Staples Center in Los Angeles.

It was clear to Ben – and to me – that at the final media events Wilder was feeling the pressure of the biggest night of his career, when he'd be fighting against the lineal heavyweight champion of the world. He was seeking confidence by making statements that were not true, such as saying that I couldn't handle the conditions at the Big Bear training camp and that I hadn't genuinely beaten Wladimir Klitschko back in 2015, that I somehow didn't deserve the decision. Wilder was experiencing the kind of pressure that he had never had to deal with before because I was by far his most dangerous opponent yet. I was totally confident that I could pull off the shock of the year but I was equally secure enough in my own skin that I could say that Wilder was unbelievably dangerous. As the fight got even nearer, these feelings eventually brought with them a sense of serenity – a calm assurance that eventually suffocated the moments of dread. The sickening feeling subsided and was suppressed by my complete belief that there was not a man on the planet who could handle what I could bring to the ring.

Of course, there were always going to be concerns within my team because of the time I had spent out of the ring, and the fact that I had only boxed twice, against moderate opposition, in my comeback. So there was a bit of doubt about whether or not I could perform under the lights again against such a ferocious fighter as Wilder over twelve hard rounds, which was understandable. In the build-up, Wilder kept taunting me, saying that he was going to knock me out, and he believed it, but I wasn't affected by him. As I said to him at one of the press conferences, 'If you're the man to knock me out then fair play to you, and I'll shake your hand. But I've travelled the world many times and fought many different champions, and I've never been knocked out.'

Paris got into Los Angeles four days before the fight and I was very happy to see her because we had been apart for eight weeks while I was in camp. We were then joined by some of my cousins, who flew in from Australia and whose visit added to the sense of the occasion. The fans were pouring in, too. With every day more and more arrived from the UK. By the time of the weigh-in, twenty-four hours before fight night, LA was buzzing.

Just before that, and with three days to go before my date with destiny, my dad broke his vow of silence and called to wish me well for the fight. He said he knew my fighting spirit would see me through. It was a good moment for me. He hadn't spoken to me over all the weeks of training because when my dad says he'll do something, that is that. But he's a father and he had to make the call. I can't remember him changing his mind too often in the past once it was made up, but he did on that occasion, and it meant a lot.

The weigh-in was to be held outdoors, at the front of the Los Angeles Convention Center, and I was going to make sure that I arrived in style. I was the heavyweight king and LA was going to know about it. From the moment I left the hotel I stood up through the sunroof of our long black car and roared to everyone who could see me for the next three miles that I was here to show everyone who was the number one boxer in the world.

The Americans had not seen anything like it – here was this giant British heavyweight screaming from a car, and they were lapping it up. Other cars were blasting their horns and screaming, 'Gypsy King! Gypsy King! Gypsy King!' By the time I got to the weigh-in there were 6,000 fans chanting, 'There's only one Tyson Fury!' Wilder was supposed to be the home fighter but I was the one getting all the cheers and backing. I had received good support when I fought Wladimir Klitschko in Germany, but this was even better; a lot of the Americans were behind me too. In the previous few days I had encountered many,

many locals coming up to me saying, 'Hey, Tyson, do the business, man.' They knew me, but they didn't know their fellow countryman Wilder. They had connected with my comeback story but they also remembered me from when I had been on HBO when I defeated Klitschko. Wilder had never been on such a stage.

When we did get to the stage I soaked up the roars from my supporters and unloaded another verbal assault on Wilder, who stood on stage hiding behind his Bane-style mask. I weighed in at 256½ pounds and he was 214 pounds. The fight was on. I was less than twenty-four hours away from completing my journey back from the brink of suicide to WBC heavyweight champion of the world – and the number one in the division.

That evening, as I was preparing to go to bed, I stepped out on to the balcony of my hotel room and looked up at the Hollywood Hills, contemplating how far I had travelled in such a short space of time. I also thought about the task that was awaiting me in the shape of Deontay Wilder, who had stopped every man he had ever faced. I didn't believe God was going to allow that run to continue. During the last fortnight I had been receiving short inspirational verses from the Bible from a friend back in the UK, which bolstered my confidence in God. I had my final prayer on that balcony, praying to God that he wouldn't allow me to falter on fight night.

As I lifted my eyes up, I saw a beaming cross in the distance — it was the same kind of experience that my dad had had the night before I fought Klitschko. I was rocked back, and then within the blink of an eye I felt at peace. I've never had a better night's rest than I had that night, and when I woke up on 1 December there wasn't a shred of doubt in my mind that I was going to complete my mission.

The same could not have been said about those around me. It's not a criticism, just an observation, that I could feel some of their apprehension. When I spent time with Paris, although she didn't say anything, I could feel that she was nervous, and why wouldn't she be? She had heard all the doom-mongers insisting that I was going to be flattened, and she was aware of my dad's real concerns about me taking the fight so soon in my comeback. Ben was a little on edge too, and he admitted to praying to God for a sign that all would be well. Like me, he saw a sign: just after he had prayed the sun broke through the clouds and hit the side of his face.

As the hours counted down on the day of the fight, I was chilled out. I went for a walk and returned to my hotel to relax with the team until it was time to go to the arena. I arrived at the venue two hours before fight time and as usual one of my team, Asgar Tair, who has been part of my inner circle for years, had all of my gear laid out and the music playing. We were listening to some country music – Chris Stapleton's 'Tennessee Whiskey' was one of the tracks he put on. It was hardly the usual kind of music that boxers listen to before a fight, and when the WBC commissioner came in he asked, 'What's going on in here?' I made him laugh as I joined in a little singalong with the team. For me, the fight doesn't really happen in my head until I'm about to go into the ring. Then I know what I have to do. I'm able to flick a switch and completely go into fight mode. But when I'm in that dressing room I'm not nervous, not at all. Waiting there for the Wilder fight I felt ready; I was just kicking back before the call to fight.

· · ·

Back home in Manchester it was a different story for my dad. Having worried that I wouldn't come home the same man I was when I left for LA, he had nevertheless booked the fight on BT Sport Box Office. But for some reason, when he tried to tune into the channel he couldn't get it to come on. He was cracking up; no matter what he tried he couldn't figure it out. Thankfully, he was saved at about 2.30 a.m. when he got a call from my mother's brother Othea, who had rung to ask how he thought the fight would go. Othea told my dad to head round to his place so that they could watch it together, and he didn't need telling twice. He jumped in the car and drove twenty-five miles so that he wouldn't miss the first round. Little did my dad know that this was not going to be the end of the drama for him.

Ben and I spoke briefly as we got close to fight time and I rested my hands on his shoulders. I told him that I would follow his instructions without question. Then my team, which consisted of my friend and chef for the training camp Tim Allcock, my brother Shane, my trainer Ben, Asgar and my training partner and friend Isaac Lowe, had a group prayer. Finally, there was the knock on the door. It was time. I could feel the tension rise in the dressing room and then I started up the chant of 'We are Spartans!' Shane shouted in my ear, 'This is what you've been waiting for your whole life; you were born for pay-per-view in America; this is your time.'

The tune went up for my ringwalk and I led the chants of 'Fury's on fire, Wilder is terrified, Fury's on fire!' As I walked into the arena, head held high, I embraced the atmosphere and sensed support from every corner. When I got to the ring I stepped over the ropes – most fighters duck underneath them but at 6 foot 9 they're a lot easier to step over. Once in the centre, I stood there waiting for Wilder, reminding myself that God hadn't brought me back to desert me at this moment; that was not how this story was going to play out. Wilder eventually paraded into the ring with his demon-like mask on. He claims to be somebody else, an alter ego, when he comes to fight. He calls on a spirit that is not the Spirit of God; not the God that I worship.

The great announcer Jimmy Lennon Jr introduced us, bellowing, 'Ladies and gentlemen, it's Showtime!', and that whipped the crowd into a frenzy. Wilder was introduced first and got a mixture of boos and cheers. Then my name was called out and it was clear who had the greater support. The roar went up for me and I screamed into the TV camera. It was a special feeling to be thousands of miles from home and yet have such passionate support.

· · ·

The bell rang . . . and then we were fighting. Despite my best efforts to talk smack to Wilder and to throw him off guard, with every block I felt the full power of his punches through my gloves. Of course, leading up to the fight I had heard about Wilder's power and his very high knockout percentage, but I still wasn't sure quite how lethal he really was. Well, now I knew. I thought, 'If that's what it's like to get hit by a jab, I don't want that right hand of his to catch me!' I had sparred with all of the top heavyweights, but I simply hadn't believed all the hype about Wilder. After the first round I understood. Like Ali knew against Foreman after the first round of the Rumble in the Jungle, when Ali realised that he would have to rope-a dope Foreman because of the champion's ferocious power.

Still, at the end of the first round I raised my hands and jigged around in Wilder's face, showing him that I was in control, that I was the man in this fight. I still had the courage to scream at him, 'Is that all you've got, Bomb Squad? You ain't nothing.' I had hurt him badly with a right hand and he had buckled. When he went back to his corner he complained to the referee that it was an illegal back-of-the-head shot – and that would hurt – but it wasn't. It was a clean shot to the temple. In contrast, when I returned to my corner, Ben was very happy with how it had gone. Things continued to go well in the second. I stuck to my boxing style of counter-punching and won the round. Only at the very end of the three minutes did Wilder catch me with a good right hand, but after the bell I just shrugged and shouted, 'Ya dosser!' Wilder may have had raw power in spades but I knew that I had the better boxing ability and the ringcraft to outfox any fighter. From there, I was able to settle down into the fight, utilising my superior skills to neutralise his attacks, slamming my jab into his face and whipping over right hands. I was defying the odds, doing my trademark slipping and sliding, and making believers out of all those in the arena and watching at home on TV who had thought that I was there to be blown away. By the sixth round I could see in Wilder's eyes that he was struggling to cope with my style and I landed some of my best punches, ramming home lefts and rights.

But I couldn't become complacent or switch off for a moment because the danger was always there. Staying within range was going to be a serious mistake and I recall that after one round, I can't remember which, Ben was telling me that although I had won it, he wasn't happy because I was getting 'a bit greedy', and by that he meant that I was waiting too long trying to land some of my own big shots.

For the next six rounds I continued to confound the critics, producing a performance for the ages. I grew and grew in confidence, and I could feel that Wilder was getting more and more desperate with every passing round. Despite a knockdown in the ninth, when Wilder tagged me behind the ear, I wasn't hurt and I could feel that I was having the better of nearly every exchange. I knew I was on the cusp of one of the greatest comebacks in boxing history. At the end of the tenth round I roared, 'Come on! I'm the Gypsy King, I will be victorious!'

But the victory would have to wait for another day. Two rounds later, I was flat on my back. Wilder exploded a right hand and then caught me again with a left hook as I fell to the canvas. The referee was counting me out. Wilder had his back to me and was doing a victory dance, thinking it was surely all over. I was finished . . .

. . .

Five seconds later the comeback was alive, the darkness gave way to light as I rose to my feet. It was all meant to be, whatever has happened in my life. I was supposed to go down against Wilder; I was supposed to rise dramatically. Yes, Wilder caught me with a good shot, and fair play to him. He had every right to think that the fight was over and that the Gypsy King was done for. But when I looked back at the video footage after the fight, and saw the shock in Wilder's eyes as I hauled myself up, ready to fight again, I knew it was divine intervention. Wilder couldn't believe it; the world couldn't believe it. Even the referee Jack Reiss, who said I opened my eyes around the count of five, couldn't believe it.

In the dressing room before the fight Jack had said, 'If you get knocked down, I'll ask you to move to the right and then move to the left to show me that you're all right.' So when I got back up after Wilder's big right hand, I put both hands on Jack's shoulders and said, 'I'm OK.' He asked me to move this way and that, and that's what I did.

The fight restarted and Wilder went in for the kill, catching me with another left hook, this time a harder shot than the one that had put me down. Miraculously, I stayed on my feet this time and then I hit Wilder a few times. Referee Reiss would later tell Ben that in all his time in boxing he had never seen anything like it. He said to Ben, 'The man was out cold and then to somehow get back up and finish stronger than the other guy was just unbelievable.'

I actually don't remember getting hit for the knockdown. But after Wilder had floored me with that right hand in the final round, I knew instinctively that that moment represented everything that I stood for, and everything that I had been through over the past few years. I also knew that it was God's will and decision for me to rise from the canvas at that moment. It was to demonstrate His power and to show people around the world who are struggling in life that there is a way out of the deepest pits of helplessness.

Once I was back on my feet, relying on my fighting spirit and survival instincts, Ben was trying in vain to get his message across to me from the corner. He found himself being pinned down by three officials as he screamed and shouted, unable to get up to the ring to see if I was all right. He was naturally concerned about me as his fighter, and yet incredibly the officials were not giving him the opportunity to see how I was. It was mayhem in and outside the ring. The next thing Ben did see when his wrestling match with the officials ended was me putting my hands behind my back and taunting Wilder, which had him screaming, 'Nooooo!' Ben wanted me to hold on and to stay away from Wilder until the final bell, but instead I took Wilder on and made him miss, before I slammed him with a right hand and a left hook of my own.

My boxing heart and confidence couldn't even be dented by the heavy blows that had sprawled me out on my back just a minute earlier. I was now the one in the ring working hard, throwing punches. As the final bell rang I raised my hands in triumph before jogging across to jump on to the ropes to salute the fans who, as one, hailed me as the victor, and hailed one of the greatest comebacks that the sport of boxing has ever seen.

My brother Shane ran into the ring and his eyes filled up with tears. He hugged Ben in delight and I could see how much it meant to them that we had completed our mission. It never crossed our minds that the decision could be anything other than a win for me. I think even Wilder's own team knew that they were beaten. His trainer Mark Breland seemed to leave the arena before the verdict was announced, and Lou DiBella, a key member of Wilder's team, came into the ring and told me that I had won the fight. But somehow the Mexican judge Alejandro Rochin scored the fight 115–111 to Wilder. Canada's Robert Tapper had it 114–112 for me and then, of all people, the British judge Phil Edwards ruled it 113–113 and so the fight was declared a draw. Everybody at ringside was shaking their heads in disbelief. The crowd reacted with a chorus of boos. The respected analyst and former world champion Paulie Malignaggi insisted I won by nine rounds to three; Floyd Mayweather pointed to me as the winner.

I was the winner but the record books will say that I drew with Deontay Wilder. Ben was naturally fuming; I've never seen him so angry. He thought I had been robbed of a glorious moment that could never be repeated and he was in a rage. But I knew that I had to keep my cool. I knew that I had to take the decision with good grace, otherwise there was a genuine threat of a riot because emotions were running high. How one judge scored it for Wilder and another judged it as a draw, I will never know. After all I'd been through, part of me couldn't believe that I had been robbed in America like this. One man who had predicted a draw was the former undisputed world heavyweight champion Lennox Lewis, who was at the fight working for television. He had suffered his own highly controversial draw in 1999 when fighting Evander Holyfield for the undisputed title at Madison Square Garden. Most believed he was a clear winner and he would eventually win the rematch. For some reason he felt the same thing was going to happen to me in LA. 'Tyson Fury won the fight,' said Lennox, before stating that I was 'miles clear' on his card.

But, you know, the draw was meant to be. I got more credit for the draw than if I had won. People will remember that moment of me getting off the canvas in the twelfth round in the Staples Center for as long as boxers put on gloves. The fact is that was Wilder's chance to beat me; that was the chance for any boxer to beat me because I had been out for so long and I came back with two easy fights.

A year on from weighing about 28 stone I was fighting the fearsome WBC heavyweight champion . . . I was beating him, then I got put down with his best shots, and I still got back up. That fight was a message to anyone who has their individual struggles. It was a beacon of hope for those who feel that their inner demons have them by the throat. It demonstrated what is possible, even when you have hit rock bottom. What unfolded that night in LA was the biggest victory ever seen in a draw.

CHAPTER THIRTEEN

FAMILY VALUES

Walking into the packed press conference in the Los Angeles Staples Center after our epic encounter, I was filled with a sense of accomplishment and of fulfilment. Together, Deontay Wilder and I had shown everyone, without a shadow of a doubt, that we were the top two heavyweights in the world. The heavyweight division hadn't seen a night like that for years, so it was appropriate that when I stepped up to face the media I spread my arms out wide like Russell Crowe in the movie *Gladiator* and roared, 'Are you not entertained?' This brought a great response from the room, and it was clear from the questions just how much the members of the press had appreciated my performance, and to a man they believed I was the victor.

I had really enjoyed the twelve-round battle. Wilder proved that he's a good fighter but if he is honest with himself, he should tell the truth and admit that I won the fight. But he can't admit it to himself that I won. Everybody knows what happened; they know the truth. Never mind not being able to finish me off in the twelfth round, even in round nine he had two minutes and thirty seconds to finish me when I was a wounded animal and he couldn't do it. The Gypsy King was on top of the heavyweight scene once more.

Wilder actually refused to come to the press conference after the fight. Instead he wanted his own press conference, and I think that was because, as a fighting man, you know when you've lost – and he knew he had been beaten. He knew that in front of me he couldn't make any excuses, but without me there he could say what he wanted and he would not be challenged, and that's what he did.

Interestingly, ever since the fight there has been no contact between Wilder and me. Before the fight we were texting back and forth, good and bad stuff, lots of amusing banter. But afterwards he went silent. I even texted him after Anthony Joshua had turned down a huge sum of money to face him, and told Wilder that if he offered me the fight, I wouldn't turn it down. Three weeks after that night in Los Angeles I texted him to wish him a merry Christmas, saying, 'All the best champ and let's get this rematch done.' He didn't respond.

Wilder did admit at his own press conference that he couldn't believe that I got up in the twelfth round because he couldn't have hit me any harder. Well, they do say you can't go swimming without getting wet. And I got drenched! Still, I left the press conference, after leading a rendition of 'American Pie', with a sense of accomplishment. By the time we all got back to the hotel I just wanted to go to bed. All the effort and emotion of the fight hit me and I crashed out. The next morning I chatted with a few friends and then headed to the airport to fly home.

Obviously, part of me was disappointed with the decision. I still couldn't believe how anybody could not have scored the fight for me – it was just baffling. But I carried with me a very different emotion going home to the one that I had felt after defeating Wladimir Klitschko. There was no sense of darkness or depression kicking in. If there was a time when I could have fallen back into a black hole then it would have been there and then. I did think to myself that everybody would now be expecting me to drift back into depression after working so hard to drag myself back to the top of the sport, only to be robbed at the moment of triumph. But because I was now an ambassador for mental health I was determined to prove that no matter how many times you can be put down in life, no matter how you have been hurt or how badly you have been treated, you must continue to fight back and you can overcome the worst that life can throw at you.

As a point of contrast, before the Klitschko fight I was asked what I would do after I won. My response was simple: 'I will probably be depressed for a very long time.' I knew the black clouds were coming and there was nothing that I could do about them.

But now returning home after the Wilder fight my mindset was completely different and my outlook on boxing had changed dramatically. Before, I would have read absolutely everything about the fight – analysing every aspect of it and studying it obsessively. This was because back then I had put my heart and soul into boxing. It wasn't a job, it was my life, and because of that, when I had gone through my dark days, it was as if a part of me had died when I didn't box. But now, I saw boxing for what it was, it was my job – it was how I earned money to feed my family and to pay my bills. It was not personal any more between me and other people in boxing. Before, a promoter could have said something about me and I would have got right on to Twitter to have a real go back. But now I didn't really care because I knew it was their job to promote their fighters. Now I understood it as business.

Social media can be such a tidal wave of negativity and I know now that it's not good for me to be near it. I've overcome a big hurdle in my life and I don't need to be part of that world, which brings a lot of people down and leads them to judge themselves against other people. It can be horrible and I've no doubt that it is a major contributory factor in leading people to have serious mental health issues. When I look back at some of the photos and the interviews and some of the things that I said back then when I was ill, I know that a person who was well wouldn't have acted like that. So my advice to someone who is ill around you? If they do outrageous things, you shouldn't think that their behaviour is embarrassing – they probably need professional help. My family had originally looked at me and wondered what there was for me to have been sad about, and they were like 'pull yourself together'. But that was probably one of the worst things that they could have said to me. It wasn't their fault, but they've since learned to have a much better understanding of what mental health is all about.

As I got off the plane back on home soil, my dad was there to meet me. After embracing me and telling me how proud he was of my performance, he insisted that we had to go somewhere before I could go home – straight to the hospital in Liverpool. Dad had been shocked with the way I had got up after being smashed down on to the canvas by those Wilder bombs and he wanted to make sure that I was all right, that everything was fine inside my head. So we went to the hospital and I had an MRI scan. Thankfully everything was OK. But that's my dad, and that's a side that the public doesn't always see of him because he can be so animated when he speaks about me, and about how great a fighter he believes I am. There has always been a deep concern that we've held for one another. We have never needed to say a lot to each other; my dad and I just know that when the chips are down we can count on each other. That's a father–son bond.

My brothers have been with me along this road, too, and the one who has been the closest to me has been Shane, simply because we are only a year and a half apart in age. Shane is someone who is always concerned; he is eager for me to show my best, and he believes in my ability so much that he wants to see me beat everybody up in each fight and look a million dollars every day. But since my comeback I have learned that I can't always be on top form. As a fighter you get tired, you get hurt and you get run-down. During the build-up and the training camp for the Wilder fight my brothers accepted this, and helped create a sense of calm and belief for me. They give off a naturally positive vibe. Shane was there for seven weeks of the camp and my younger brother Hughie came in for the last two. I know that during the fight itself, Hughie was an emotional wreck; he could hardly watch, he was praying most of the time. He would look up for a minute and then put his head down. Hughie actually said to me after the fight, 'That's enough, just walk away. I can't take any more. You've done it all now, there's nothing more to prove.'

Paris was in a worse state and couldn't get over what she had witnessed that night. She not only told me to retire but she also didn't feel that she could sit through another fight with me against Wilder. In the immediate aftermath, she felt so ill and when she got back to our hotel room she ripped off her false nails, wiped away her make-up and sat on the bed, crying for three hours. It was horrible to see my wife go through that kind of trauma and I'm sure there are many wives and girlfriends of boxers who can relate to that experience, because they know the fine line between a glorious night in the ring and a tragic one. Through the tears, Paris didn't hold back: 'I don't want you fighting again, Tyson. It's too hard, it's not worth it!'

The emotional roller-coaster that Paris, Hughie and my family went through illustrates how much they care. That's the depth of love and concern that few others in boxing can really have for a fighter. Everyone else is doing a job and if the fighter loses, well, they just move on to the next show. With regard to the management team and the promoters, if I lose it's a case of, 'Oh well, bad luck' but it's not the end of the world to them. They move on to the next promotion. But my family, they don't get any money from it so for them it is everything. It means so much – there's family pride and love on the line every time I step through the ropes and into the ring.

With Shane, he had always given it to me straight.

He's not a yes man and I respect that. After the Wilder fight he told me, 'I don't make a living off you. I've got my own money so I don't want anything from you.' If he has something to say about a certain matter, he has always hit me with it. Like my dad and me, Shane and I feel genuine concern for each other. If one of us fell into the sea with no hope of survival, we'd rather jump in and die with each other than accept the reality of no hope. When I think of our relationship today, it really goes back to our childhood. When Shane and I grew up we spent a lot of time with our mother because my dad was a workaholic and would regularly leave the house at seven in the morning and would not return until eleven at night. Dad had a reputation for being a hard man back then and he was tight with his money, so we would always ask my mum instead for pocket money and she would give in, offering us treats and taking us on trips to Blackpool. She was always very supportive but to this day she has never been to one of my fights, either amateur or professional.

To be honest, my mum doesn't fully understand what I have achieved as a boxer. I took her out shopping one time after the Wilder fight and I was being stopped for photographs and autographs everywhere I went in Manchester and she couldn't understand it. She actually said, 'Hey, son, how do you know so many people?' I had to explain to her that I was the heavyweight champion of the world and a lot of people had watched me and supported me. That day was actually very special. It was a lovely time that I spent with my mum – just like any son would like to do. I was able to treat her to her favourite perfume and I wanted to buy her a Louis Vuitton bag, but she ended up shouting at me, 'Don't be wasting your money on that. Save your money because you never know when you'll need it!'

Only a mother would tell off a multimillionaire like that. She was more worried about me than about herself and I guess that's the way all good mothers are; I'm in awe of them. When I look at my mum, while I am a natural fighting man, I do see some of her character in me as well. I was thinking a lot about this kind of thing after the Wilder fight. How had my family made me the man I was; how did they shape me to succeed in my toughest moment?

I believe the work ethic I have as a fighter and as a person goes right back to my 89-year-old grandmother Patience. She had never had much money, she'd had a tough life, but she instilled in the hearts and minds of my brothers and me the essence of working. As a young boy I would help her clean and do some jobs for her. She had grown up in London and she used to tell me that even as a teenager she would have been out helping her father with his job tarmacking roads. She showed me old photos and I learned a lot from her; it was very educational how she brought up my father and her other sons. It wasn't about material gain but about how important it was to graft, and to be ready to fight in life because it could be hard. When your grandmother laid roads as a teenager, I suppose there has to be real grit in your genes! And I'm sure that has helped me in the ring. It's that same work ethic that I will try to give to my own kids. It would be too easy for them to become lazy and to live off their father, but I know this won't happen. Their dad won't be around for ever and they need to have the same work ethic that I do so that they can achieve their own dreams.

After the Wilder fight, the more I thought about my upbringing, and how it had defined me, the more I realised that there were other family members who had helped me, too – even if I hadn't realised that they were doing it at the time. I think my work ethic developed further after I spent time as a teenager in Torquay with my aunt Ramona – my mother's sister – and her husband James, who was a landscaper. I loved going down there because, as they had no children, they would spoil me rotten. I would do the work, picking up rubbish and waste, carrying out some labouring, and then after work I would head to the beach to swim, or to play some cricket. It was a very different lifestyle to what I was used to, but I found it very refreshing and I learned so much. In fact, I would go so far as to say that if it wasn't for them, I wouldn't be the man I am today. Ramona and James taught me to work hard and to appreciate the good things that you are blessed with. James was a man who worked extremely hard but he also had a real style, which I admired, and I like to think that his sense of style rubbed off on me.

I remember he had this beautiful Bentley and he would wash it every day. He would chamois and polish it, and take great pride in its appearance. He also took great pride in his own appearance and I'm definitely the same. To this day I like to stand out in a fine suit and to be well groomed. James always looked smart and was always well-tanned, and that was different to the men I had grown up with, who were a bit more rough and tough and more down-to-earth. I liked the style that James had and I guess it's down to him that I like to bring some colour to my wardrobe.

Ramona was an interior designer so she had a great touch in terms of giving a property the wow factor. Ramona and James would go to auctions and I'd join them. As with my dad and his car business when I was growing up, buying and selling was clearly going to be in my blood, and would put me in good stead for selling my fights.

· · ·

When Christmas 2018 arrived, I had sold my biggest fight of all – the fairy-tale comeback against Deontay Wilder – thanks to all the innate characteristics instilled in me by the various members of my family.

It was a Christmas to be savoured, the complete opposite of 2015 and the depression that set in after beating Wladimir Klitschko. The real Tyson Fury wasn't going away this time. The heavyweight division now knew that the King was back and he was here to rule for as long as he wanted.

CHAPTER FOURTEEN

A NEW DAWN

Philadelphia, 2007

Instinct took over and told me that this was the wrong place, the wrong time. It was my first time in America, and the first – and only – time in my life when I had found myself running away from a fight. But when a 9mm or a switchblade was about to come my way, I think I made the right choice – and it still seems like it was the wise decision.

I had travelled to Philadelphia as an amateur with the Ireland team, which included some top prospects like future world bantamweight champion Ryan Burnett and Steven Ward, a world-rated light-heavyweight. This was around the period when I had given up on my dream of boxing for Great Britain at the 2008 Olympics and decided to follow my Irish heritage.

Once we had arrived in the city, with some time on our hands, my cousin Phil, who would also go on to box professionally, and I decided to go out for a walk. We didn't know where we were going; we were just chilling out. But as we turned a corner this guy jumped us and told us where to go. At first, I thought to myself, 'No way', but when we realised that our lives were probably on the line, the two of us took off like Usain Bolt. We got back to the place where we were staying, shaken up but in one piece. We explained to the Americans who were looking after us where we had been and we immediately saw the look of shock on their faces. They went on to explain to us that we had somehow found ourselves in one of the most notorious gang areas in the whole of Philadelphia, and that the guy who was ready to take our lives probably assumed we were two rivals trying to take over his turf. My first time in the States and my career could have ended right there and then.

Instead, only a couple of days later, I made the first of a few big impacts I've had in America, when I was matched with Maurice Byarm at the famous Blue Horizon venue, where they filmed the first *Rocky* movie. I was very proud to wear the Irish vest as I made my way to the ring in a packed arena, which was anticipating a good scrap. The Irish Americans were going nuts as they saw me step through the ropes. Byarm had been doing a bit of trash talking leading up to the fight, saying that he was going to knock me out so hard that my 'momma would feel it back home thousands of miles away'. That, as you can imagine, just helped me to get fired up even more for my first fight on American soil. I wasn't going to allow this big mouth to get the better of me. I was going to show the Americans what the future heavyweight champion of the world looked like.

Byarm, who was a southpaw, was a good bit smaller than me but he clearly fancied himself as the new Mike Tyson because he came right at me throwing left and right hooks. I was able to tie him up in the early stages and then I got to work with my left jab and straight right hands. However, as I caught him with an uppercut he landed a left hook and that got the crowd going. In the second round, I surprised him with my hand speed and a left shot to the body that had him complaining to the referee. I was now in control and Byarm knew that he was behind, so he came out bobbing and weaving, swinging bombs at the start of the third and final round. I stayed calm and as he backed up into a corner I landed one of the best hooks I've ever thrown. As he sagged against the ropes I landed another hammer right hand that sent him crashing to the canvas. Looking back today, it was a finish not too unlike the way I would put away Steve Cunningham at Madison Square Garden years later in 2013, which would be the next time I boxed in the States.

The reaction from the crowd at the Byarm fight was incredible. Here was this big Irish heavyweight, tall dark and handsome (even if I say so myself!) knocking out their man in style. With so many Irish Americans in the crowd, they especially loved it. Former world heavyweight champion and boxing legend Joe Frazier was at ringside because he had helped arrange the competition in conjunction with his son Marvis, who had also fought for the world heavyweight title. They asked me about the possibility of staying in the States longer term. The funny thing was that me and my cousin Phil were already seriously considering running away to America, leaving the amateurs behind us and trying to make it as professionals in the US, because we loved the whole vibe of the place. We were just teenagers but it seemed like a good idea. Phil was keener than me so his eyes widened when it was suggested that we make the move after the buzz I had created with the win at the Blue Horizon. But I was starting to go out with Paris at the time, I had my family back home and when I sat down and thought about it with a cool head it just wasn't for me. However, it was clear the Americans liked my style and I loved being around them.

· · ·

Over a decade later, and having journeyed along the professional ladder, I knew that I was still made for the American stage – I just needed the opportunity. The seeds had been sown with my 'victory' over Deontay Wilder in December 2018, but unbeknownst to me, they would bear fruit in 2019, and grow to a level I couldn't imagine.

Having returned home from Los Angeles and reflected on the controversial draw with Wilder I was content that I had made a huge statement to the world. That clip of me climbing off the canvas in the twelfth round was seen millions of times on social media. Everyone wanted to see the rematch; it was going to be the biggest, most lucrative fight in world boxing and the talk behind the scenes started immediately. I was expecting that it wouldn't be long before I would have a date for the second bout. While there was some speculation of bringing the fight to Wembley Stadium in the spring or summer, which would have been unforgettable, to be fighting in front of my home fans in London, the reality was that Wilder was still the champion and his team were likely to insist on a venue in America. That didn't bother me because I knew that when and where wouldn't matter; when I did face Wilder again he was going to take a beating.

My coach Ben seemed to be taking the draw with Wilder harder than I was. As soon as the fight was over, he had messaged the team at BT Sport asking when they could send him a copy of it so that he could watch it again. When they did send it over he was watching the fight over and over again, trying to get his head around how all three judges could not have scored the fight in my favour. It was constantly on his mind and he reckons he eventually watched it a hundred times, trying to discover any little things that we might have done differently. Fortunately for him, he had booked a holiday in Orlando and New York with his girlfriend Esra for shortly after the fight, and that managed to calm him down and take his mind off it. He went from wondering what we could have done better, to seeking to understand even more flaws in Wilder that could be exposed the second time around. Ben now believes that there were a few things that we could have done better that night. But he also thinks that all reflections on that fight in Los Angeles have to be grounded in the context of what I had come through in such a short space of time.

After Ben returned from his trip we reconnected in the new year. I couldn't have been happier and Paris was expecting our fifth child. At the same time, I was acutely aware of just how important it was for me to stay in shape because that helped me so much in regard to my mind remaining in a good place. I also wasn't sure when the call might come for the rematch with Wilder and I wanted to make sure I was ready. Ben felt that, too, and we agreed that it would be good to take another trip to Marbella for a three-week training camp.

On New Year's Day, when a lot of people I imagine

were probably getting over the festivities from the night before, Ben, Esra and me and the family headed out to Marbella. I soon had the sun on my back once more and good people around me. I loved training every day. It wasn't as serious as the previous twelve months because I was still waiting on word of my next fight, but it kept me ticking over. In fact, Ben tried to rein me in a little because he felt that I was working too hard but I was just enjoying it so much. I even had a bit of fun when we took a couple of kick-boxing classes that a local instructor was running. I showed the class that I could use my feet to good effect as well. And of course, because I love a challenge, I threw down the gauntlet to all twenty students that I would spar two rounds each with them, kick-boxing. And I did, with every one of them. That was great fun. The topic of Wilder came up now and again, and Ben and I reflected on how that twelfth round would perhaps live on in boxing history for years to come.

I was receiving plenty of media attention back home in the UK, and in a positive way too, and I was entering a new year as I had never done before. Just twelve months earlier I had been in the same place in Marbella losing so much weight, but now I didn't have that same mountain to climb.

When we arrived home I enjoyed taking the kids to school in the morning and playing with them at the weekends. I was keen to get some word on the Wilder rematch, but then came some news that I didn't see coming. I received a phone call from my friend and former world champion Amir Khan to tell me that America was calling me louder than ever before.

Amir said that the leading promotional company in the world, Top Rank, were interested in doing a deal with me. Top Rank is run by the legendary promoter Bob Arum, who worked with such great fighters as Muhammad Ali, George Foreman, Sugar Ray Leonard and Oscar De La Hoya – all box-office, household names. And now, to my great honour, he was interested in doing a deal with me. Many of his previous fights had been shown on HBO, but he now had a deal with ESPN, and their internet streaming channel, ESPN+. After thirty years, HBO had shut down their boxing operation as the way boxing was being televised was changing in the States. Eddie Hearn had done a big deal with DAZN, which is a company that streams sports on a subscription basis, and the ESPN+ channel is now their direct competitor, along with Showtime, who continue to put on pay-per-view events for the very big fights, in the same way that Sky and BT Sport do in the UK.

I knew that ESPN was a big platform in the States, going out coast to coast into so many homes, bars and hotels, but I wasn't interested because I had just fought on pay-per-view on Showtime against Wilder and felt that my profile had shot through the roof.

But then I got a call from my management team MTK Global about the possible deal with Top Rank and ESPN, and they outlined how they wanted to make me an American star. That part didn't actually matter to me, because I'm not interested in being a celebrity. It just doesn't do it for me. If I wanted to, I could probably go to hundreds of celebrity nights every year. But it's not my thing. I'm a normal person who has just been lucky and done all right through boxing. So that wasn't going to be a motivating factor for me. However, they also said that I could have a couple of fights and then look to do the Wilder rematch. Initially, I still wasn't that interested because I felt that I would have been happy just with the Wilder rematch and then I could hang up my gloves and move on to another chapter in my life.

But as I weighed up the biggest offer I had ever received in my career – enough money to set my family up for life – along with the fact that I would have such a powerful American promoter behind me, I felt that it all started to make sense. And I would get my shot at the American dream, after all. I agreed to sign with Top Rank in February. Frank Warren and BT Sport would continue to organise my affairs in the UK but Arum would be leading the way in the States. With this news, when Frank was asked about the negotiations for future fights with the big names in the division, such as Wilder and Anthony Joshua, he said, 'They will now have to come to us. This ESPN situation is probably one of the biggest things to happen to a British sportsman. It's something special.'

I was the lineal heavyweight champion of the world – the unofficial 'true' champion, often referred to as 'the man who beat the man' – and now I had the kind of promotional backing on both sides of the pond that such status deserved. As the WBC champion with the backing of Showtime, Wilder understandably felt he could call the shots, as did Joshua, who at the start of 2019 was the WBA, WBO and IBF title holder and had the backing of Sky and DAZN in the States. But this deal I did with Top Rank turned everything my way. I was completely in control of my destiny now, and the financial clout behind me was a match for anyone in the heavyweight division.

With the multimillion-pound deal agreed, it was now a case of where I would start my new American adventure. I quickly decided with Top Rank that there would be no better place than Las Vegas. The venue was going to be the famous MGM Grand hotel and 15 June the date. Wilder and his team, who assumed I would be going for the rematch right away, got the shock of their lives when they saw how much Top Rank were getting behind me and so they decided to make other plans as well. Wilder would be heading to New York in May to face Dominic Breazeale, who had been knocked out by Joshua in seven rounds, a month before my date in Vegas. In between that, Joshua was pencilled in for a defence against American Jarrell Miller, but after Miller failed a drugs test, Mexican Andy Ruiz stepped in to face him on 1 June at Madison Square Garden. The heavyweight world was on fire like it hadn't been for about twenty years, since the days of Mike Tyson, Evander Holyfield, Riddick Bowe and Lennox Lewis.

It was decided that I would be fighting unbeaten German Tom Schwarz on my Vegas debut. Ben had seen Schwarz box in Germany in March as he had been over there with another boxer and so he suggested him to Top Rank and they agreed.

When Bob Arum said he was going to make me a huge star he certainly meant it, because from the moment I hit America I was on every major television chat show. We touched down in New York and had a meal with the Top Rank team and then for a few days I was part of a media frenzy. On the chat shows I was very open about the troubles that I had been through and the mental health issues that I had overcome to return to the ring, and that really seemed to connect with people. I would be opening up about the despair I found myself in and

245

I could see the cameramen and women with tears running down their faces, and it was the same with the audiences. Afterwards, some of the TV people, including some of the presenters, would approach me to talk more about their own experiences. I was touched. And although it was not something that I had chased, I have to say that I did appreciate the warmth and the respect that I was receiving from the American public. In return, I tried to repay that warmth and respect to every American I met.

I still had to make sure that I was preparing properly for 15 June and so early in the mornings I would go running with Ben in New York, with the Statue of Liberty right beside us. That somehow felt appropriate because I felt as liberated as I had ever been in my life. The shackles were off and I was about to compete on the boxing stage that I always felt I was born to perform on. Next stop, Vegas.

Tim Allcock, who is a key member of my team, organised a house for us in Vegas for the four weeks we were staying there and that worked out well. When we did take a walk down the Strip it gave everyone a bit of a thrill and a buzz to see my face plastered all over the place, and lighting up the billboards. Ben's only concern was that because there wasn't the same edge of danger surrounding this fight with Schwarz, compared to the clash with Wilder, that I could possibly underperform.

But I knew that I was here to put on a real show, before, during and after the fight.

As we arrived in Vegas, Wilder had just taken care of business in New York with a first-round knockout of Breazeale. It was a sensational stoppage and it was a case of 'over to you, AJ' as Joshua got ready to defend against Ruiz, a chubby Mexican who had lost on points to Joseph Parker in 2016 when challenging for the WBO title. (Parker would eventually lose his belt to Joshua.)

As the whole team sat down to watch the fight we, like just about everybody else in boxing, were expecting Joshua to retain his titles quite comfortably, but that changed when I saw him making his walk to the ring in Madison Square Garden. Both Ben and myself immediately felt that there was something not quite right because Joshua looked cold, and by that I mean that there wasn't a bit of sweat on his body. Before any fight, as a boxer you go through such a good warm-up that there's sweat glistening from your body as you leave the dressing room. But that wasn't the case with Joshua. He looked nervous; he looked like he didn't want to be there. And after previously thinking that he would win on points, I turned to the lads and said, 'He's going to get knocked out.'

This was the first time Joshua was in a big fight away from his home country and when that happens you react in one of two ways – you either feel out of your comfort zone and shrink, or you rise to the occasion. If you're totally confident in your ability you'd be happy fighting in outer space. When I go to the ring, I'm there to fight, no matter what is in my way – it's as simple as that. I bring my heart to the ring every time. But in New York against Ruiz, it just seemed like Joshua had left his heart back in the dressing room. Joshua was a 1/25 favourite and he knocked Ruiz down in the third round. But then in one of the all-time biggest shocks, Joshua himself went down twice in the same round before being knocked down repeatedly again in round seven when he was stopped on his feet, having spat out his gumshield after hitting the canvas. As the referee waved it off, a few of us jumped and shouted, 'He quit! He quit!' He seemed to have given in. It was shocking to see the way the fight ended. To me, it was no surprise that Joshua struggled to recover after being put down, because any time he has been hit in his career that has been the case. But this time he seemed happy to lose. That's something that I can't comprehend, a concept that's alien to me because I'm not bred that way – there's no quit in me. The little fat guy beat the body beautiful and the heavyweight division was turned upside down.

Just like Joshua, I was a huge favourite going into my fight with Schwarz two weeks later. There was a lot of expectation because the whole event was based around me but I embraced it and I had a special ring entrance all prepared for my new American fans. I thought I would take a leaf out of the *Rocky IV* script by donning the same Uncle Sam gear that Apollo Creed wore when he came in to face Ivan Drago. To add to the sense of occasion, I had the James Brown hit 'Living in America' blasting out from the speakers, and the showgirls doing their thing as I made my way to the ring. The crowd went crazy for it. A year on from my comeback fight against Sefer Seferi, I was in great shape and ready to give ESPN and all the fans watching a night to remember. When I was growing up, my dad always had the big fights in Las Vegas on TV and I would get up in the middle of the night to join him and watch fighters like Floyd Mayweather and Naseem Hamed. Ricky Hatton was always my hero growing up, and here I was headlining in Vegas and he was in my corner as part of the team. It was a special night.

But I still had a job to do and it seemed to be overlooked that Schwarz was unbeaten and ranked number two by the WBO, particularly when that organisation had ranked me at number four. I knew how hungry he would be, and I knew how he must have felt to have been written off, like I had been before so many big fights – against Wilder, Klitschko and further back to my first fight with Dereck Chisora. Yet on that night in Vegas I would have smashed anybody. I felt so sharp and so focused on giving a spectacular display.

After strolling into the ring with the Stars and Stripes hat and shorts on, I delivered a show to match my entrance. Credit to Schwarz, he came and he had a go but I took him apart. Two of my shots in the second round smashed up his nose, and then with a minute to go he came charging at me and I showed off my defensive skills. As Schwarz threw eight straight punches, I made him miss with every one of them, and then responded with a nice little body shot of my own. About ten seconds later Schwarz was on the canvas for the first time in his career, from a fast right hand. He got up but he was finished and as I unloaded, the referee called a halt with six seconds remaining of the second round.

I know that going into the fight Ben had wanted me to use my boxing skills to gradually break down Schwarz, but I just wanted a devastating performance so I was heavy-handed from the opening bell. I held my feet more firmly so that I could generate more power and everyone saw the effect. I had added a little extra weight as well, and my punches were damaging. I know how well I can box and I can use my defensive skills when I need them, but this was a night to show people that if I have to stand and trade and have a war, then I'm ready. Because I have the dynamite to do serious damage when called upon.

I spread out my arms in celebration as the fans went wild. At ringside my promoter Bob Arum couldn't keep the smile off his face. As he said to me afterwards, 'You couldn't have written your first night in Vegas any better.' In the ring, to finish off, I sang to Paris the same Aerosmith song I had sung to her after I had defeated Klitschko – 'I Don't Want to Miss a Thing'. When you go to Vegas you have to entertain and that's what I did. Bob said that I was a mixture of the second coming of Muhammad Ali, and George Foreman during his amazing comeback when he took the heavyweight title from Michael Moorer at the age of forty-five.

But as far as I was concerned I was just Tyson Fury, the Gypsy King, because I don't believe there has ever been a heavyweight like me. I was there to have fun and I enjoyed every moment of fight week in Las Vegas. It was pure entertainment from start to finish and that's what the fans had wanted. The reaction from ESPN was terrific: the viewing figures were great, and social media went crazy for my ring entrance and the finish to the fight. In the press conference afterwards, Bob was already talking about the rematch with Wilder breaking all box-office records: 'When the time comes we'll help sell it but we have the best salesman sitting between us,' he quipped as we sat addressing the media. The entertainment continued right up until the end of the press conference when I even got Frank Warren and Bob Arum to join in as we sang 'American Pie' to close the Vegas experience. Bob admitted that in all his fifty-five years' experience of boxing he hadn't seen anything like it, and he certainly hadn't been part of a trio at the end of a press conference!

The after-party was held in the Hakkasan restaurant inside the MGM and there were around 4,000 fans in there, with 200 VIP guests. There was such a party atmosphere, and I even got on the mic and gave them a few songs before going to bed. The support I had received from the fans who had travelled over from the UK, along with the Americans who had packed into the MGM, was hugely appreciated. Off the back of the Wilder fight and this win over Schwarz, it really felt like the whole world had finally awakened to everything that I believed I could bring to the sport of boxing. But most importantly it was just a great time for my family and friends who had stuck by me throughout my roller-coaster journey. And it all seemed a very long way away from the shy little boy playing netball at primary school to be headlining in Las Vegas, so I felt very thankful that I could enjoy this time.

This was a new dawn for my career and for my life generally, because there was a real sense of purpose and direction to everything that I was doing. Not for a moment was I going to take anything for granted, because I knew more than most how quickly things can change in this business. But as I left Las Vegas on the Monday morning I believed that whatever else I wanted to achieve in boxing, the opportunity was going to be presented to me – and I was certainly ready to grab it with both fists.

· · ·

The path to a second fight with Deontay Wilder was clear, and word came through quite quickly that it would continue in Vegas. My new promoter Bob Arum was working hard behind the scenes with the Wilder camp to see how and when a deal could be agreed. The fact that I was now aligned with American channel ESPN and Wilder was linked to cable channel Showtime meant it could have been difficult to find a way to agree terms – a lot of big fights have stalled because of fighters being on different television channels. One of the biggest fights in history, between Floyd Mayweather and Manny Pacquiao, only happened because Showtime and HBO agreed to simultaneously screen it as a pay-per-view event.

But Arum and his Top Rank team got a deal done and Wilder and I were placed on a course that would lead to our rematch on 22 February 2020 in Las Vegas. A third fight had also been agreed because the interest in the two best heavyweights in the world going head to head was so great. With that in place, Arum set me up for a return to the ring on 14 September, at the T-Mobile Arena, Las Vegas.

My opponent was going to be another unbeaten fighter, Sweden's Otto Wallin. Even though he hadn't lost a fight and was ranked number four by the World Boxing Association and eleven by the International Boxing Federation, two of the four major governing bodies, as a choice of opponent he came in for criticism in some quarters. Often people who have not seen a fighter assume he is not up to scratch but I knew that he was a good fighter and I wasn't going to be taking him for granted. He had done a good bit of sparring with Anthony Joshua and the word around the gyms was that he had done very well.

I've learned not to worry what others say because whenever you step into the ring there are always risks. So I trained as hard as ever for Wallin and spent five weeks in a house in Vegas as we counted down to the fight. There were plenty of media and publicity commitments as there always are, and that included a joint interview with the man I had been named after, former world heavyweight champion Mike Tyson. We had met for the first time in 2016 and shared a few phone calls after that. He's a guy with his own troubles, and he's had plenty of trauma in his life that I could relate to. But the man is a living legend and I couldn't believe we were sharing laughs and opening up to each other.

In the week of the fight I embraced the fact that it was the annual celebration of Mexican independence. The Mexicans have a rich fighting history and I was keen to show my respect to them. So in their honour I donned a Mexican bandana and Lucha Libre wrestling mask for the public workout! The fans seemed to really enjoy it, and during my time leading up to the fight the Mexican people gave me such a good reception.

Everything was going to plan, and even the Mexican journalists were enjoying the Gypsy King show now as well. In a press conference I had suggested that I'd been trying to learn some Spanish and so one of the Mexican reporters decided to wrong-foot me by asking a long question. After thanking him for the question, I smiled and quipped, 'Yes, I also like big cuddly toys and crayons!', which had the room in stitches. The fight, though, was not going to go as smoothly as I hoped – far from it – and I was the one who would literally be in stitches by the end of the night.

• • •

With a poncho and a sombrero, I entered the T-Mobile Arena on Mexican Independence Day blowing kisses to the packed crowd. After two decent rounds I felt that I was in control, but then in an instant everything changed. With about fifty seconds to go in round three, Wallin caught me with a short left hook and it opened up by far the worst cut I've ever had in my career, over my right eye. My trainer Ben would later say that it was one of the worst cuts he'd ever seen, too. This was a crisis. The referee said it was an accidental head clash but then broadcaster ESPN, in between rounds, informed Ben that it had been caused by a punch. That was critical because it meant that if the fight was stopped, Wallin would be declared the winner.

Things went from bad to worse when in the fourth round I sustained another cut, this time on my right eyelid. My cuts man Jorge Capetillo did a miraculous job but from the third round onwards I was worried that referee Tony Weeks would stop the fight. The blood continued to pour into my right eye, which meant that I could only see properly out of my left. My pre-fight game-plan now went out the window, and I had to make the decision to get up close and personal with Wallin because that way the referee wouldn't have long periods to look at the cut and maybe then decide to stop the match.

All I was thinking about was getting through to the end, making sure I did enough to win each round. Wallin was now going for it, throwing the kitchen sink at me and rubbing his gloves in the cut. There was a scary moment in the sixth round when the ringside doctor took time to examine the cut. He had the right to call off the fight but I told him, 'I can see, let's go', and I got back to work.

This was a test of my character and conditioning, and I showed Wallin that even with one eye I wouldn't be beaten. At the end of the ninth round I caught him with some heavy shots and that continued at the start of the tenth. Some fighters would have gone on the defensive with that sort of damage to their eye but I took the fight to the Swede and rocked him to his boots. This is what champions do when the chips are down. I hurt him again at the end of the eleventh. But credit to Wallin, he dug deep and a big left hook caught me in the final round. I finished the fight with a sea of blood around my left eye. Wallin was exhausted, having fought the fight of his life, and the referee's shirt was smothered in my blood and sweat. Thankfully, there were no tears, and I won the fight on points with a unanimous decision from the judges. However, back home my dad John, who was working for BT Sport, was getting very emotional and at the end of the fight called for my whole team to be sacked.

It had been another night of drama and it ended with me visiting the local hospital. The cut over my right eye was so bad that I didn't have time to do any media; I had to be taken to the hospital so that it could be examined and fixed up. My cuts man Jorge had done such a good job that I gave him a bonus, but now I needed a whole team to repair the damage. I didn't just want the doctor to work on it, so we had to wait for an hour for the surgeon to come from his home. He got to work, put in almost fifty stitches and after twenty minutes it was job done. At first I wasn't sure how long it was going to take to heal properly but he told me just two weeks, which was great news because it meant that my date with Wilder on 22 February was still on.

After winning $5,000 at the casino the next morning, it was time to head back home. But it wouldn't be long before I was back in the States after I received an invitation to take part in the World Wrestling Entertainment (WWE).

I wouldn't be fighting Wilder for a while and I'd always been a fan of the WWE, the way they put on a real show for the public. So when the opportunity came I just thought, 'Why not?' We made a family holiday out of it in October, and Paris and I and the five children flew out to Orlando, Florida, to the WWE's Performance Center. There the wrestlers train and learn how to look after themselves in the ring, and I can confirm that it's a lot more intense than people would think – and pretty sore on the back!

From there we headed up to the Staples Center in Los Angeles – the scene of my fight with Wilder – to be at ringside for the WWE SmackDown. For my son

Prince it was a dream come true. He plays WWE on his PlayStation every single day and when he got to meet the superstars backstage, including The Rock, it was amazing for him. I was the best dad ever!

When we got to ringside one of the big names, Braun Strowman, gave me a stare and put up his fists, as if to say he was up for a fight. I skipped over the barricade and the sell-out crowd went wild as the security held me back. A few nights later we were at another event, WWE Raw, and after I demanded an apology from Strowman it all kicked off as we both brawled with security guards in the ring. Prince and my daughter Venezuela were loving it, too, and when the WWE announced that I would be facing Strowman in Saudi Arabia on 31 October, Prince couldn't believe it. His dad would be fighting the guys he pretends to be on PlayStation.

Before that was possible, I had to go through some rigorous training. To be honest it was brutal. I would spend a couple of hours with a special professional coach who would show me how I would have to deal with being thrown into the corners, which was like being hit against steel wire. We would work on drop kicks and other moves including being tossed onto my back. The first couple of days I came away aching, covered in bruises.

When I signed the deal with the WWE owner Vince McMahon, I thought it was just going to be a bit of fun, but I ended up working more intensely than ever because not only were we training hard but also flying all over the States. I had to base the family in Orlando, while I was getting on flights – for example, at 3am to Denver, Colorado, to promote the event on 31 October and then back to Florida before flying out the next day to Los Angeles. The schedule was hectic, like nothing I had experienced before, and I couldn't believe just how big WWE is in the States and around the world. Sell-out stadiums everywhere you go and a reputed one billion fans.

So on the horizon I had the challenge of facing the so-called 'Monster Among Men' in the wrestling ring. Then it would be full steam ahead for the biggest boxing event in the world, Fury–Wilder II in 2020.

CHAPTER FIFTEEN

BIGGER THAN BOXING

The dark cloud of depression will always hang over me, wanting to rain poison on to my head. That's the way it is going to be until the day I die. But, now more than ever, I realise why I had to go through what I did all those years leading up to, and even more so after, the victory over Wladimir Klitschko in 2015. And I also know why the battle must go on because I can now see my true purpose in this life. By the grace of God, I have been placed in a position, on a worldwide stage through boxing, to be able to help others, and that means so much more to me than what I've ever done in the ring. I'm not interested in winning more belts. I would be quite happy to walk away after another three fights and start the next chapter of my life.

In fact, this process of moving beyond boxing has already started because I have been blown away by the reaction I've had to my story, from people all over the world. The whole issue of mental health, of individuals finding the ability and the courage to admit their feelings, and the need for governments to take it much more seriously, is developing all the time. If I can play some small part in this conversation, and in helping even one person change their path in life, that would mean more to me than any victory with a pair of gloves.

I feel very humbled by how people have responded to hearing my story. I have even learned this year that my trainer Ben Davison has also suffered from depression, and that's one of the reasons why he has been so good for me during my comeback: he can read the signs in me when I'm not in a great place, and he knows exactly how to respond. Crucially, Ben has understood me. He knows how to get the best out of me in the gym, and he works hard at making sure that my media commitments don't become too much. Sometimes we will start a gym session that he has planned for that day and within five minutes he'll stop and say that's enough, because he can see that I'm just not in the right place to do what he wants me to. We'll just rest and talk, but one thing that must happen every day is that I have to train – I have to do something to keep my mind in a positive place. I also feel that when I have trained I have earned the right to eat. That's part of my medicine and it has to be taken.

An example of all of this was in the lead-up to the fight with Tom Schwarz in Las Vegas in June 2019. We had flown in late from New York to Los Angeles and even though I was tired I wanted to go and train. Ben could see in my eyes the real need for this to happen. The logical thing for 90 per cent of boxers would have been to rest and recover for the next day's training, but for me to be in the right frame of mind I had to work out. So, Ben and I went and did a light workout and that meant the next day I was ready to go and work even harder.

Ben had his own mental health issues years ago when he found it hard to get out of bed and was in a bad psychological place. Incredibly, only a couple of weeks before I called him to help me return to the ring, he was suffering from a particularly bad bout of depression. He has admitted that if I had called him then, he wouldn't have been able to train me. Ben wondered on many occasions, as I had, why he had been put through the things that had happened in his life that led him into depression. Then, with the call I made to him and the role he has played in my return to the ring and my personal journey, it has come to make sense to him.

Ben can read me like a book because he has been there; maybe not to the same extremes, and he didn't have the public looking in on his problems, but the issues were essentially the same. As Ben says, God doesn't make mistakes and the timing was right for the both of us when we started to work together in 2017.

While training is paramount to keeping me in balance, I also have an app on my phone that lets me know the number of days in a row I have read my Bible. There's a passage each day that I read and if I don't then the counter returns to zero and I have to start over again. Reading my Bible every day is very important to me and helps my state of mind in a significant way. In our Travellers culture there is a healthy fear of God and I was always brought up going to church. My uncle Ernie was a preacher and from a young age I was intrigued by the Bible, which has answers to the world's problems and sets out guidelines for how society should be. My faith has been a pillar throughout my life and has been critical in my battle with mental health. I listened a lot to Ernie's sermons at different conventions and we would sit and have long discussions about the Bible; he was a good teacher and I learned a lot from him. I know in my life I have made some big mistakes but I'm also acutely aware of the forgiveness of God. The world could do with a lot more awareness of that because it just seems that the negative judgementalism that we see in the world, particularly on social media, is sending people into a depressive state, and so many young people in particular seem to be suffering because they can't handle the criticism and abuse.

I have become very aware of just how big the issue of mental health is since I went on my speaking tour all over the UK after the Deontay Wilder fight. I met thousands of people who described exactly the kinds of problems that I have gone through. I've also received numerous letters as well as direct messages online, from members of the public and from other top sports stars and public figures. At times it has just been overwhelming, but everyone needs to know that people from every part of society are going through these kinds of problems – feeling there is no point to life, unable to see a purpose, being hit by a sense of helplessness. I want to say this again, to each and every person, that if the heavyweight champion of the world can go as low as any person can do, when he's supposed to be so tough, then it can happen to anyone. But there is a way back.

One of the most humbling and proudest moments of my life was when I was asked by Frank Bruno to become an ambassador for his foundation. Frank has gone into detail about his own struggles with mental health and is determined to help as many people as possible. To now be a mental health ambassador means so much to me. It happened around the time I was doing my talks as they have all proved to be very moving experiences. I've seen so many men and women reduced to tears as they have listened and related my story to their own lives and what they are going through, expressing their own fears and worries. I don't say this because I want a pat on the back and to be told that I'm a great fella, or that I'm the one who can help everybody, because I'm not. That's why the first thing I say to people who come up to me is that they need to go and seek medical advice. But I am touched that even people I have never spoken to before have been affected in a positive way by my story. I've had people from Africa, Asia, America and Europe fly in to some of my nights on tour and they've come up and expressed to me the impact my story has had on them, and it's a very, very humbling experience. But at the same time it makes me realise that this is my real purpose now in life. One man from Texas recently flew in for a show that I did in Manchester and he came up to me and said, 'Thank you for saving my wife's life.' Another person came from South Korea to the show in Leeds and said a similar thing, that somehow my fight against depression had inspired their loved ones to fight back.

The very concerning thing for me is the amount of younger people who are suffering in silence. Mental health is a silent killer and it needs to be brought out into the open so much more. It's very disturbing to see how young people are affected and how they feel they have nobody to turn to; like one lad I spoke to for an hour in Sheffield who stood there trembling, telling me he didn't want to live any more. Or the teenager I started speaking to on a bridge because I noticed that he didn't have a coat or his mobile phone with him and was in a desperate situation. It's shocking to think that suicides among teenagers in England and Wales have risen by 67 per cent since 2010 and it's the biggest killer of men under forty-five years of age. I feel passionately that this has to be addressed with much more vigour than ever. This is bigger than boxing, it's people's lives on the line and you don't have to do shows around the country to be aware of it. One Sunday I was in the back garden when the doorbell rang and it was this woman who was in a right state about her son, who she said was feeling suicidal and she begged me to go and speak to him. He didn't live too far so Ben and I went down and spoke to him; being a teenager he felt awkward about telling his parents something, but he felt he could open up to Ben and myself. A few days later he came to the house and gave Paris a box of chocolates and a thank-you card because that one hour chat had helped give him the encouragement he needed to get up and face the world again. Young boys and girls need people to speak to, they need specialist help so they can move forward in their lives.

Homelessness is another issue that I feel passionately about and, of course, many of those who are homeless will have mental health issues which are often the root causes of the rising problem. I saw the horror of it in Los Angeles when I was preparing to fight Deontay Wilder but it's the same right across the UK and it just can't be right that one of the richest countries in the world can have so many people without proper shelter. These are big problems for people in higher positions than me to get to grips with, but I will keep trying to play my small part and if I can continue to be an inspiration to others then that will mean the world to me.

Certainly, the public's perception of me has changed a lot since my comeback and there's not a day that goes by when I don't receive some letters of support in the post. People just write 'Tyson Fury, Morecambe, England' and it makes it to my home. Letters have come from all over the world and while I read every one of them, I sadly don't always have the time to respond to them. But the stories that people send me are heart-breaking: about how their husbands, parents or teenagers have been tortured by depression and felt that they had no way out but that listening to my story had inspired them to change.

My wife Paris has been shocked as well by the change in the public's reaction to me. Before my comeback it got to the point where she didn't want to go out in case she heard bad comments about me or someone would even confront her about something I had said on Twitter, but now she has seen how positive people are and the effect my story has had on people. It even led the great singer Robbie Williams to get in touch with me so we could record a Christmas song together. He came over to my house, we set up a makeshift recording studio and made the record.

Whereas before I would have been concerned about what I would do in my life after boxing, I no longer have that same fear because I have a purpose beyond the sport. I also feel that when I do retire I'll stay around the sport because I believe I can advise young boxers on the pitfalls and how to make sure that they get the best they can out of the sport. I know the business of professional boxing inside out now and I feel if anyone wanted advice I could give it to them. Boxing is a sport that gives kids a chance to change their lives. Look at someone like Naseem Hamed, who went from a council estate in Sheffield to becoming a multimillionaire, or the lives that Frank Bruno and Ricky Hatton were able to have because boxing can offer you rich rewards if you are prepared to make sacrifices to achieve your goals.

Yet, at the same time you could sacrifice maybe fifteen years of life and still not end up with much at the end of it. It's such a high-intensity sport, the highs can be so high and the lows so low for a fighter who loses that it is very easy for boxers to slip into a depressive state. Equally, for so many the adulation can be so intoxicating that when the time is right to walk away from the sport they are unable to do so because it is such a drug, and replacing the high of thousands of people chanting their name can be so frustrating that it leads to depression. Many fighters have spoken about this, and the problem with boxing is that when a fighter has finished his career there is no body or group to help them with life after boxing.

Other sports have a governing body that has people who can help, but boxing is such an individual sport and an unforgiving business in many ways that there is no real support mechanism to help former fighters. I'm fortunate that I have a brilliant support network around me but also that I have goals beyond my days in the ring. I will always need to train but equally I believe I can be around the sport and give something back to those who feel they need help.

It is often spoken about in sport what kind of legacy someone will leave behind, but that is not something that I am very interested in. I don't like to dwell on how people will view me in years to come because that's up to them. What I can deal with is the here and now, and that's about enjoying my accomplishments in the ring but also, more importantly, being a good father and a good husband. Paris and I are very determined to make sure that our children have good values. They can't expect to be given any handouts. It would be very easy to spoil our kids and, of course, they will grow up in a comfortable environment in comparison to many children. But if they're going to make their own way in life they will have to know that it requires hard work. We're very blessed to have five great kids. Our eldest, Venezuela, seems to have inherited my athletic genes and a bit of my showmanship as well because she's already looking like a very good runner and really enjoys her dancing, while Paris says Tyson junior is just like me because he doesn't listen to a word she says! A close family unit is worth more than gold and that's a top priority for us.

I have come to appreciate more and more the simple things in life, to appreciate my family more than ever – whether that's enjoying a lunch together or a holiday with the kids like in the summer when we were in London and it was Tyson junior's third birthday. We had his party at Shrek's Adventure! and it was fantastic. I couldn't have been any happier and yet even then there was a little reminder of how my mood can swing in a moment. We were meant to drive down to London but I just said to Paris, 'I can't do this', so we booked the train instead and it was perfect. We went to the aquarium and had a lovely time together. It was a precious moment and if I want to be remembered for anything it is being a good father and husband. Champions come and go, and they're forgotten about.

• • •

For as long as I box, and beyond that, I hope that I can continue to be a beacon of hope for people so that they can have their own 'Wilder moments' – the time when they rise from their bed and face the world again, or when they see a new purpose to life, like the guy who sent me a picture of himself at 20 stone and then one of him after he had lost 8 stone. Overcoming problems like these is far from easy, and everybody who suffers finds themselves in a unique position; what works for one person may not work for another. But there is genuine hope of making a change to their lives, and my life is a testimony to that.

My way out was to get down on my knees and cry out to God because there was nothing else that was going to free me from the despair I was in. He answered my prayer, I felt a sense of a burden lifted and God decided that I would have another chapter in boxing. I stopped the drinking and partying, teamed up with a new trainer, Ben Davison, and started the long journey back to being the fighter I knew I could be again, and more importantly back to being the person I knew I was – or should be.

I had come to terms with the depression and the anxiety I was being tortured with and everyone around me could see the difference as the months went by and I got stronger and stronger. My marriage returned to normal and I was able to be the real me. I'm far from perfect: I still have moments when my mood dips for no reason, I still say some silly things but, by the grace of God, I'm a changed man. I didn't want to put on an act any more, I wasn't going to put on a mask and play a role any more, I just wanted to be me – to be a good husband and father and to do justice to my God-given talent in the ring. I had to face up to the fact that I was in denial about my behaviour at times and the life-long fight I've had with depression.

But I want everyone to know that if I can win this fight, so can you if you seek help. To those family members suffering as they watch a loved one act in a way that is not normal, I hope they can stay in the fight too, just as Paris did for me. No matter how bleak it is, there is a way out; I know how dark it can get, but I also know there is light, there is hope, and I'm an example of that. I make plenty of mistakes like anyone else, but I'm battling on and appreciating life like never before.

USEFUL MENTAL HEALTH CONTACTS

If you think you, or someone you know, is experiencing mental health issues you should seek professional help immediately. In the UK you can contact your local GP for a full range of options with the NHS. Below are some leading mental health organisations who are also on hand to help.

The Frank Bruno Foundation

I am proud to be an ambassador for The Frank Bruno Foundation, which aims to provide Non-contact Boxing alongside Wellbeing programmes for adults and young people who are facing or recovering from mental ill-health issues.

The Frank Bruno Foundation is a direct result of Frank wanting to give something back to the community. Frank has faced challenges both in and out of the ring and has always done so with determination, dignity, humour and humility. But it is Frank's bravery and honesty in talking about his battles with mental health issues which continue to earn him the respect of those whose affection he won as a boxer. It is fitting then that supporting sufferers of mental ill-health is where Frank feels his attention is best focused.

For more information, visit
https://www.thefrankbrunofoundation.co.uk/

Mind

Mind is one of the UK's leading mental health charities. They believe no one should have to face a mental health problem alone. Whether you're stressed, depressed or in crisis, they'll listen, give you support and advice, and fight your corner. And they'll push for a better deal and respect for everyone experiencing a mental health problem.

For more information, visit the Mind UK infoline:
Call 0300 123 3393 or text 86463 or visit
https://www.mind.org.uk/

Samaritans

Samaritans offer people a chance talk to them anytime in their own way – about whatever's getting to them.

Going through a difficult time? You can contact Samaritans FREE on 116 123 (support available 24/7).

For more information, visit
http://www.samaritans.org/

PROFESSIONAL
BOXING RECORD

Statistics

Name   Tyson Luke Fury

Nickname(s)   Gypsy King,
The Furious One,
2 Fast

Date of Birth   12 August 1988

Nationality   United Kingdom

Division   Heavyweight

Stance   Orthodox

Height   6″ 9″ / 206cm

Reach   85″ / 216cm

Professional Fight Record

Date	Opponent	Venue	Belt	Result
14 September 2019	Otto Wallin	T-Mobile Arena, Las Vegas		Win. Unanimous Decision
15 June 2019	Tom Schwarz	MGM Grand, Las Vegas	World Boxing Organization Inter-Continental Heavy Title	Win. Technical Knockout
1 December 2018	Deontay Wilder	Staples Center, Los Angeles	World Boxing Council World Heavy Title	Draw. Split Decision
18 August 2018	Francesco Pianeta	Windsor Park, Belfast		Win. Points
9 June 2018	Sefer Seferi	Manchester Arena, Manchester		Win. Retired
28 November 2015	Wladimir Klitschko	ESPRIT arena, Dusseldorf	World Boxing Association Super World Heavy Title International Boxing Federation World Heavy Title World Boxing Organization World Heavy Title International Boxing Organization World Heavy Title	Win. Unanimous Decision
28 February 2015	Christian Hammer	O2 Arena, Greenwich	World Boxing Organization International Heavy Title	Win. Retired
29 November 2014	Dereck Chisora	ExCel Arena, Dockland	World Boxing Organization International Heavy Title EBU European Heavy Title Vacant BBBofC British Heavy Title	Win. Retired
15 February 2014	Joey Abell	Copper Box Arena, Hackney Wick		Win. Technical Knockout

Date	Opponent	Venue	Belt	Result
20 April 2013	Steve Cunningham	Madison Square Garden Theater, New York		Win. Knockout
1 December 2012	Kevin Johnson	Odyssey Arena, Belfast		Win. Unanimous Decision
7 July 2012	Vinny Maddalone	Hand Arena, Clevedon	Vacant World Boxing Organization Inter-Continental Heavy Title	Win. Technical Knockout
14 April 2012	Martin Rogan	Odyssey Arena, Belfast	Vacant BUI Ireland National Heavy Title	Win. Technical Knockout
12 November 2011	Neven Pajkić	Event City, Manchester	Commonwealth Heavy Title	Win. Technical Knockout
17 September 2011	Nicolai Firtha	Kings Hall, Belfast		Win. Technical Knockout
23 July 2011	Dereck Chisora	Wembley Arena, Wembley	Commonwealth Heavy Title BBBofC British Heavy Title	Win. Unanimous Decision
19 February 2011	Marcelo Luiz Nascimento	Wembley Arena, Wembley		Win. Knockout
18 December 2010	Zack Page	Pepsi Coliseum, Quebec City		Win. Unanimous Decision
10 September 2010	Rich Power	York Hall, Bethnal Green		Win. Points
25 June 2010	John McDermott	Brentwood Centre, Brentwood	Vacant BBBofC English Heavy Title	Win. Technical Knockout
5 March 2010	Hans-Joerg Blasko	Huddersfield Sports Centre, Huddersfield		Win. Technical Knockout
26 September 2009	Tomáš Mrázek	The O2, Dublin		Win. Points

Date	Opponent	Venue	Belt	Result
11 September 2009	John McDermott	Brentwood Centre, Brentwood	BBBofC English Heavy Title	Win. Points
18 July 2009	Aleksandrs Selezens	York Hall, Bethnal Green		Win. Technical Knockout
23 May 2009	Scott Belshaw	Colosseum, Watford		Win. Technical Knockout
11 April 2009	Mathew Ellis	York Hall, Bethnal Green		Win. Knockout
14 March 2009	Lee Swaby	Aston Events Centre, Birmingham		Win. Retired
28 February 2009	Daniil Peretyatko	Norwich Showground, Norwich		Win. Retired
17 January 2009	Marcel Zeller	Robin Park Centre, Wigan		Win. Technical Knockout
6 December 2008	Béla Gyöngyösi	Nottingham Arena, Nottingham		Win. Technical Knockout

INDEX

TF indicates Tyson Fury.

LIST OF ILLUSTRATIONS

Plate Section 1

p.1 © John Fury.

p.2 © Tyson Fury.

p.3 Top left: Public Domain. Top right: © John Fury. Bottom: © Tyson Fury.

p.4 © John Fury.

p.5 © John Fury.

p.6 © MEN Syndication.

p.7 © MEN Syndication.

p.8 © MEN Syndication.

Plate Section 2

p.1 Top: © Reuters. Bottom: © PA Images.

p.2 © Leigh Dawney.

p.3 Top: © Getty. Middle & Bottom: © Reuters

p.4 Top: © Tyson Fury. Middle: © Getty. Bottom: © Sky Sports.

p.5 Top & Middle: © Getty. Bottom: © Reuters.

p.6 © Getty.

p.7 Top: © C1 Media/ BT Sport. Middle & Bottom: © Getty.

p.8 Top: © Getty. Middle: © Reuters. Bottom: © Tyson Fury.

Plate Section 3

p.1 © Tyson Fury.

p.2 © Tyson Fury.

p.3 © Tyson Fury.

p.4 © Tyson Fury.

p.5 © Tyson Fury.

p.6 © Tyson Fury.

p.7 © Tyson Fury.

p.8 © Getty.